THE INSPIRED LIFE METHOD

The step-by-step guide for How to Find Your
Life's Purpose, Heal Your Trauma and Create
a Life You Love

Lewis Huckstep

Published by Automatic Authority Publishing & Press House,
Newcastle, NSW, Australia.

Tel: +61 417 785 921

www.automaticauthority.com

First published in Australia in 2024

Copyright © 2024 Lewis Huckstep

A catalogue record for this book is available from the National Library of Australia.

ISBN: 978-1-7636510-4-3

Table of Contents

INTRODUCTION

CHAPTER 1
The Inspired Life Method   1

CHAPTER 2
Self-Mastery   15

CHAPTER 3
Your Calling: Finding Your Life's Purpose   43

CHAPTER 4
Your Quest to Conquer   59

CHAPTER 5
Dream Life and Income Needed   75

CHAPTER 6
CashFlow Quadrant and Selecting the Right Vehicle   81

CHAPTER 7
Master Planning   105

CHAPTER 8
Unlimited Motivation   125

CHAPTER 9
Inner Healing   133

CHAPTER 10

Dissolving the Ego - Remove Limiting Beliefs   161

CHAPTER 11

Balancing Perceptions - Heal Trauma   189

CHAPTER 12

Meditation - Remove Blocks   231

ACKNOWLEDGEMENTS   263

About the Author   265

INTRODUCTION

I've been inspired to write this message for a long time. Something inside has consistently brought me to think about, talk about and finally be here, writing this life-changing guide. We shall go on this journey together to reveal your **True Authentic Self** and **Purpose** that is deep within you – who you are without wearing the 'masks' or the personas you present to the world. You will be guided every step of the way as we:

- Reveal your True Authentic Self.

- Discover your life's calling (Purpose).

- Overcome all trauma, mental or emotional limitations that are self-sabotaging you.

- Gain absolute clarity of the steps you need to take to create a life on your terms from a practical level.

By the end of this book you will have created your own step-by-step Master Plan to be able to create your Life's Vision. You will have constructed a 'toolbox' of strategies and methods that will allow you to heal from any unhealed trauma (yes, we all have trauma), because until you do, your trauma will continue to be the silent puppet master that controls your behaviour.

You will go through the Purpose Process, revealing what your life's Purpose is, and no, you don't need to do years of therapy, go meditate on a mountain or take psychedelic drugs to find this (though I am a fan of all three). In this book are all the ingredients that you need to live a meaningful, fulfilling life.

I really want to drive something home for you right now by telling you that this book can be the ultimate resource to inspire you to create a life to be truly proud of.

You can break free from those toxic patterns, those limiting beliefs, that self-sabotage and the internal judgement over yourself and others. All the lack of motivation, the volatile emotional swings, the addiction to external stimuli (drugs, TV, social media, the accumulation of things), the destructive Ego, not living in the present moment, and living with anxiety and depression will all be things of the past.

This guide will take you through **The Inspired Life Method**, which is broken into three important pillars:

1. **Self-Mastery**
2. **Skills and Strategy**
3. **Inner Work**

These pillars build on each other and, once you have read through them, they are designed so you can go back and revise whatever section you feel you need as a refresher.

This is my invitation to you – let go of the attachment to who you think you are. Let go of who you think you need to be in order to be 'enough' to receive love. You are exactly where you are supposed to be, reading this book right now. You have arrived here at the perfect time, ready to absorb the lessons and growth this guide is going to provide for you.

Let me be clear – while this is not a motivational book, completing the activities in it will motivate you. This is a practical and spiritual guide to allow you to create the life you are worthy of. My invitation is to fully engage in the exercises and get ready to grow.

I will share very honest and vulnerable parts of myself to give you context and real examples of how everything we go through, especially the painful experiences, shape who we are today.

When I was younger, some family members weren't who I 'wanted', but they were exactly who I 'needed'. I don't have hatred or negative energy towards them – quite the opposite. If it weren't for everything I experienced, I wouldn't be here now sharing my story to serve others. I have done a lot of work on healing from my childhood and I'm grateful for everything that I went through. My journey has made me the man I'm proud to be today. In this book, I am sharing some of the tools I've used to do my own healing, so you can either begin or continue your healing journey.

The Inspired Life Method was created to help my younger self when I was at my lowest. Back then I didn't know who I was or where I was going, and I struggled to manage my mind and emotions. Emotional breakdowns, self-sabotaging patterns, not allowing people to get too close to me in intimate relationships and achieving status goals because of insecurities – these were all the norm for me. When I didn't have the parents/mentors I wanted and needed, when I was at my most vulnerable. This is for you, young Lewy.

PS: Due to the levels of depth that *The Inspired Life Method* goes into, and the tools I use to teach this with my clients, some exercises have been shortened and moulded to suit the purpose of this book. If you want to experience the full depths of the Method, you will find ways to do so towards the end of the book.

Let's begin.

CHAPTER 1

The Inspired Life Method

I pulled the phone away from my ear, I dropped to my knees and started crying. *I'm fucked,* I told myself.

Seven years of 'hustle'. Seven years of showing others how 'successful' I was externally, yet still feeling 'not enough' internally. Twenty-two years of wearing a mask to protect myself from being hurt. It all came to a beautiful, destructive end... I had received many 'awakening' moments in my life, and this was definitely one of the biggest.

My relationship was on the rocks. My bank account gave me anxiety every time I thought about opening it. My self-worth and confidence were at an all-time low. My friendships were non-existent or very shallow at best. I had built a life where I tried to show the world how happy and successful I was, but deep down I was really hurting.

I was 22 years old and I had opened three gyms. My fuel of choice to get me there was my insecurity– feeling like I wasn't enough and trying to earn my dad's love/approval (we'll come back to this in later chapters). I had sacrificed my health, friendships, intimate relationships, life experiences and enjoyment ... all so I could look successful. *So smart!* But as life (the Universe) always does, it had a big lesson on the way for me and–it was during a phone call that I received it.

My three gyms all relied on me. I thought I had built successful businesses, but instead found myself trapped in a very stressful job that didn't pay well with businesses that were barely profitable.

My business partner at one gym didn't see eye to eye with me, so we decided it would be best to sell. After finding a buyer, we went through the selling process for a whole year of back-and-forth negotiations. At the same time, I was working 16 hours a day to keep all the businesses alive. I lived off four to five hours of sleep a night and I constantly had stress and anxiety-fuelled fights in my personal and professional life. I also neglected my physical and mental health. In short, life sucked. My only lifeline to get out of this was selling the business. I was desperate for it.

After we eventually signed the sale agreement, I felt free ... kind of. Now I had only two unsuccessful gyms, an unfulfilling relationship, my unhealed trauma, an unrepaired relationship with my dad and a bank account that still gave me anxiety. Yay!

Then the phone rang, and when I saw the buyer's name pop up on the screen, my heart sank. I answered and could feel the tension through his voice within seconds. My gut tightened. I knew something bad was about to happen. "Mate, this business is not what you told us it was. We're pulling out of the deal." I dropped to the ground in tears. I had hit my breaking point. I could not see a way out. *I'm fucked*, I told myself, *I should just shut all the gyms down. Georgia* (my partner) *is going to leave me. Why would she want to be with someone like me? I don't want to wake up tomorrow to this same bullshit. I'm tired of fighting. I can't keep doing this.*

I called my business partner straight away. "What do you want to do?" he asked. My response was one of fear and stress: "I can't do this anymore. You can have my shares of the gym," I told him. I'd spent years building it from the ground up, but I couldn't handle the life I'd created for myself any longer. He accepted my shares, so I was free of one of the gyms.

Very dark, challenging months followed. I got little sleep and often napped at the other gyms during business hours. My relationship with Georgia was going backwards, I was living in fight-or-flight mode daily, and I was running on a low battery. Looking back, I'm surprised I got through it.

However, that time led to a shift in how I viewed the world. It forced me to look within, to address a lot of the unhealed wounds I was ignoring, to get clear on what my life's Purpose was and how I wanted to fulfil that Purpose (I knew then it wasn't owning gyms). With the gift of hindsight, I realise now that I was missing many pieces of life's puzzle, and I needed those pieces to have a life that inspired me.

It took two more years to sell the second gym, to scale myself out of the final gym and to get to the point where I made $2000–$3000 a week from just one hour of work. This gave me the time and opportunity to lean into my Purpose more, to do an even deeper exploration of myself, and get completely clear on the life I wanted to live and how I was going to make that happen.

The biggest lessons I took away from this period of my life were:

1. I wasn't clear on who I authentically was. I was wearing a mask to impress others and hide the parts of myself I felt ashamed about. I didn't know my Values or my Purpose. It was like having a car with no fuel.

2. I didn't know what I truly wanted. I was chasing goals without the intrinsic drive required to attain them. I didn't know my Mission or Vision. Like driving a car but not knowing my destination.

3. I lacked a plan of how I could go from where I currently was, to a life that I was truly inspired to create. Like driving a car with no map to follow.

4. I lacked the skills that I needed to create my Dream Life. Like not even knowing how to drive the car.

5. I also recognised that my unhealed trauma was 'self-sabotaging' me from being able to live and create the life I wanted. Like I was repeatedly forcing my car to go in the wrong direction.

That breaking point I'd experienced was the wake-up call I needed. It forced me to work on the personal and professional growth required to build a life with time and financial freedom. This then allowed me to pursue my dreams: To build a deep, conscious, intimate relationship with my partner; to get in the healthiest shape of my life; to heal through my unhealed wounds; to be who I authentically am without all the masks, and to be able to do what I love and get paid to do it.

Unconsciously, I was piecing together *The Inspired Life Method* and that is what this is all about – my chance to share with you what I learned.

The Inspired Life Method

This method gives answers to many of the questions that cripple most people:

- What do I want to do with my life?
- Why am I so unmotivated?
- Why do I keep sabotaging my life?
- Where do I even start?
- Who am I?
- What's the meaning of life?
- What am I here to do?
- Is this all life has to offer?
- Why do I get triggered?
- How do I stop doubting myself?
- What actually makes me happy?
- How do I heal from my 'stuff'?
- What do I need to do to achieve my goals?

- How can I be my authentic self?

And the list goes on! But, once you have understood and used every single piece of this method, I am confident that you will be able to say:

> *"I know who I authentically am. I know what my life's Purpose is. I have absolute clarity on what my Dream Life is, and I have a clear plan on the exact steps I need to take to get there. I have all the skills that I need right now, and I know which skills I need to learn for the future. I have all of the mental and emotional tools needed to allow me to heal and navigate any problem that life throws my way at any time on my journey."*

If that isn't worth the price of your attention to work through this book, then maybe it isn't for you. But you want things to change, and you've come this far, so maybe it is.

Let's have a look at the method itself and its three pillars:

Figure 1

I have made a video to walk you through *The Inspired Life Method* in extra detail if you want to dive even deeper into it. To watch the video, please go to: www.lewishuckstep.com/book or scan the QR code below.

Let's break this down step by step so you understand the importance of every piece of this method:

1. Self-Mastery

Why this pillar first? Because if you're a human, you're – at some level – wearing a mask. This means you're not actually being your True Authentic Self, which in turn creates quite a lot of problems:

You will never feel whole or truly fulfilled if you try to be someone else. You'll constantly be trying to fill a void that's unfillable, and that's a very exhausting and miserable way to live.

If you're not being your real self, you'll set goals based on someone you're not. You'll be chasing goals that aren't even meaningful to you. So, you'll do one or some of the following:

– Self-sabotage those goals.

– Achieve those goals but still not be happy. (As I did with my gyms.)

– Build a life based on someone you're not and that isn't authentic, so you'll experience a crisis where you wake up and ask yourself, "*Is this all that life has to offer?*"

We solve these problems of self-mastery in three steps:

1. Determine your Values. These are the areas of your life that are intrinsically most meaningful for you. If you're unfulfilled in life, I guarantee that you are not prioritising your Values. This

sounds simple but, as you'll learn in the next chapter, most people have a very incorrect interpretation of Values.

2. <u>Discover your Purpose</u>. Your Purpose is your gift to give to the world and it's what intrinsically drives you the most in life. This is a very special process that I'm so excited to take you through.

3. <u>Craft your Mission and Vision</u>. This gives you the clarity of what your inspired future life looks like. It also gives you a measurable goal that you'll use to create your Master Plan.

I hope I've got your attention ... and that's just the first piece.

Let's continue.

2. Skills and Strategies

This is the broadest pillar of the method. Because of this, this pillar gets the least attention in this book. You'll hear this line later on, 'Success in any area of life is 80% psychology and 20% strategy/skills.'[1] The mindset (psychology) is more important than the skills and this is why most of this book focuses on the mindset. However, without the skills needed, you'll be like a person running east looking for a sunset. No matter your mindset, you'll never get the result you're after if you're doing the wrong thing.

What we will be covering in this book, however, is <u>The Master Plan</u>, which is a very detailed breakdown of your Mission/Vision into an actionable plan. We use your five to ten year goal (Mission) then break it down into: three-year goals, two-year goals, one-year goals, three-month goals, one-month goals, one-week goals and daily outcomes (Daily Huddles). All of which will give you the confidence and clarity needed to take action towards your Mission and Vision. Here's a bird's eye view:

---

[1] Tony Robbins, "The Psychology of a Winner," Tony Robbins, accessed September 2, 2024, https://www.tonyrobbins.com/stories/coaching/the-psychology-of-a-winner/

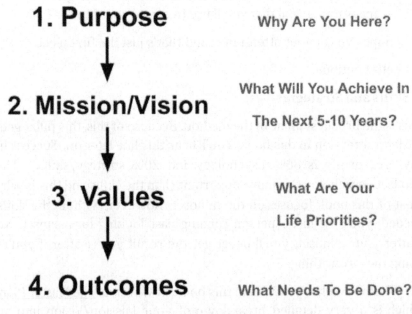

1. Purpose   Why Are You Here?

2. Mission/Vision   What Will You Achieve In The Next 5-10 Years?

3. Values   What Are Your Life Priorities?

4. Outcomes   What Needs To Be Done?

Figure 2

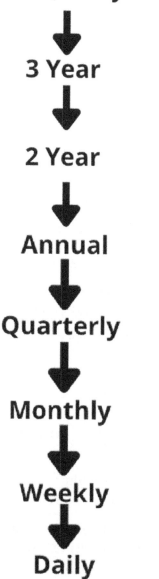

Figure 3

Doing this process really makes your dreams become reality. I can't wait to take you through it. In case you're wondering what the 'Technical Skills' and 'Soft Skills' (referred to on Figure 1.) are, here we go:

Technical Skills: These are specific abilities and knowledge related to a task. It's all the practical skills you learn through education and experience.

Examples: Developing an app, data analysis, fixing an engine, running a social media ad, squatting in the gym, cooking a meal, building a system.

Think IQ: Intellectual intelligence.

Soft Skills: These are your people skills, how you interact with others and your environment. It's the intuitive skills you develop through education and experience.

Examples: Communication, leadership, influence, decision-making, empathy, problem-solving, critical thinking.

Think EQ: Emotional intelligence.

3. Inner Work

This is my favourite of all the pillars – you'll read why later – and is the one I will focus on most in this book as we dive deep together. Inner Work is **dissolving/healing the wounds and blockages that are masking your true self**.

There are so many reasons why this is important, but I'll give you a couple before we explore more of this topic later in this book:

- Your outer world is a reflection of your inner world. You don't see things the way things are, you see things the way YOU are. If you're an angry person, you see anger. If you're a hurt person, you see danger and hurt. If you're a grateful person, you see opportunities and abundance. As you change the way you view the world, the world you view changes.

10

- Your unhealed wounds are the silent puppet master controlling your unconscious actions. You can't be held accountable for something you're not aware of. If you keep self-sabotaging your personal or professional life, I guarantee you have something internally that hasn't been healed yet.

- The more you heal, the more authentic you become. When you have unhealed wounds, you will put up walls (a mask) to protect yourself from being hurt again. However, this actually suppresses and hides your True Authentic Self. So, as you heal more, you put more walls down and express more of your True Authentic Self. Inner Work ties directly into the 'Self-Discovery' pillar.

I will guide you safely to experience three healing tools/modalities, so you can do your Inner Work using this book. I will also give you plenty of resources, so you can continue your healing journey.

This is a very powerful method. It allows anyone, at any point of their journey, who may have some or none of these pillars in place, to be able to create a life that truly inspires them. On page 266, I have created a 'final copy' for you to fill in your answers, as you progress through this book. I will be referring you back to this page many times, so keep it handy.

Before we get into the method, let me introduce you to someone who increased her sales from $3000 a month to $100,000 a month within 60 days WITH NO SALES TRAINING ... interested?

Julie was in a really dark place when we connected. She felt hopeless, she was extremely anxious and wanted to find herself and her Purpose. She was already such a talented woman with so many skills and strategies, but she really lacked the 'Self Mastery' and the 'Inner Work' part of the method.

She was in a sales role where she had previously been successfully closing over $50,000 in any given month, but in the two months leading up to connecting with me, she hadn't been closing anything. Her confidence and self-esteem had completely disappeared. She struggled setting boundaries for herself both in her romantic relationship and her professional life. She also had a lot of resistance to having tough conversations with people.

Working with Julie, it was very clear that she was pouring from an empty cup. She wasn't being selfish so she could be selfless, she was **being the best version of her limited self**. So, we put the missing pillars of the method in place and BANG ... an instant shift within herself and in all areas of her life:

- When we started working together, her sales went from $3,000 in January; to $15,000 in February; and then $100,000 in both March and April. Not bad at all.

- She set and enforced healthy boundaries in her personal and professional life.

- Her relationship improved with more love, intimacy and passion.

- She is happy and fulfilled with the life she is living.

and so much more!

See how much your life can change if you just add in the pieces that you're missing? Pretty epic.

To show you that I'm not just making up a fake person to make my work sound good, scan the QR code below or visit the link to view Julie's video testimonial:

https://youtu.be/b0yqader9XY?si=rvlLkn0zu2dElAmC

Now that you understand the power of the method, I guess it's time to go through the method yourself. Strap in, this is going to change your life forever!

CHAPTER 2
Self-Mastery

*"I saw the angel in the marble and
carved until I set him free."*

– Michelangelo

A father failed to achieve his life's dreams, and so he forced his son to live them out for him, killing the boy's own dreams in the process. Ethan was a very bright, talented boy, both mentally and physically, who had dreams of being a performer and pursuing an acting career on Broadway, and eventually making it in Hollywood. Every night before bed, he read biographies, watched videos and studied successful actors who had chased their dreams. It was an obsession he couldn't cure.

On the other hand, when his father, Bruce, had been younger, he'd had dreams of being a successful footballer. He was talented enough and had the discipline required to make it professionally. Unfortunately, his family went through financial hardship at a critical time for his athletic career, which forced Bruce to go straight into a full-time job to help support them. Without investing the time and energy needed to fulfil his dream of becoming a professional athlete, Bruce ultimately became someone who 'could have made it' and never lost that sour taste of 'what if'.

Fast forward 30 years to find that Ethan had more natural athletic talent and gifts than even his father had shown. The son won all junior football competitions as the captain and made the national teams for all his age groups. The whole town knew Ethan could go all the way. Bruce saw the potential and the chance he wished he'd had. He knew that his son could achieve – with the right resources and opportunities – what Bruce himself had missed out on many years before.

However, Ethan started to express his interest in the arts, attending auditions, getting lessons, and singing and performing around the house. Bruce's frustration and disappointment started to build. He started to have firmer conversations with Ethan. "Son, you're only young once, you can only have this shot while your body allows you to, you _need_ to take this opportunity while you can. You can do the acting stuff later." This became a regular conversation around the house.

Ethan, who idolised his dad, started to feel guilty for disappointing the man he loved the most. He stopped attending auditions, he stopped taking lessons and started to focus more on the athletic career his dad had not had. But the more he prioritised his dad's needs ahead of his own, the more Ethan beat himself up and felt guilty. His self-worth declined and his mindset became negative. Though the voice in his head was always luring him towards his true passion, he kept reminding himself, _I shouldn't be thinking about my acting career, I can't let my dad down._

This went on for years until the end of high school, and that critical time when bigger life decisions are made. Ethan had a really close friend, Brad. They had been best friends since they were eight years old. They knew everything about each other and could always tell when the other person was off. Most importantly, Brad never pressured Ethan to be an athlete like Bruce and the rest of the town did.

Brad's dad, James, happened to be a very wise personal development mentor, who also knew Ethan very well, and James and his son could see the challenge Ethan was facing between pursuing his dreams and pleasing his dad.

Ethan had received offers for fully paid scholarships from the top five colleges in the country, and Bruce had already told the entire family and the whole town about the offers, so everyone was messaging and calling Ethan to congratulate him on his 'success' before he had even decided what to do. He felt sick and unable to make a decision.

Even though he had been focusing most of his time on his football training, he still kept up with his connections to the arts community. He had managed to attend meetups and to participate in local performances, but he hadn't told his dad. Instead, he had lied and told him he'd been going to Brad's house.

Ethan had also built a relationship with a professor at an arts college, who saw Ethan's pure love for acting and knew that with the right guidance, he could have a good career as a performer. The professor had organised a spot for Ethan at the interstate college where he worked. It wasn't a scholarship so Ethan would have to work full-time to pay his college fees, but he would have the opportunity to pursue his true love.

When it came to the day he had to make a decision about his future, Ethan's family and the whole town were waiting for him to decide which of the football scholarships he would accept. Ethan was very conflicted. He didn't want to upset all who loved him by throwing away an opportunity that millions of people dreamed about, but he also knew where his heart belonged. He decided to give Brad's dad a call.

After a 15-minute conversation, in which he explained everything to James, Ethan asked, "*What should I do?*"

The mentor responded, "You can either let your own dreams die, or let your father's dream die. But there's only one person who will be with you for the rest of your life. In a thousand years from now, every single person you know, including yourself, will be dead, so anything you decide to do in the big scheme of things, doesn't matter. With the very short life you get to live, you should listen to your own inner voice. What would you love to do?"

It was exactly what Ethan needed to hear. He thanked James gratefully and went to see his family.

With his heart pounding, clammy hands and an overpowering feeling of fear, Ethan announced to them, "This is an incredibly hard decision for me to make. There are so many people who have sacrificed so much for me to be in the position I am today. However, my biggest fear is getting to the end of my life, having regret for not following my heart and pursuing my dreams. Ultimately, I know deep down that you all want what's best for me, and for me that's doing what I love rather than what people think I should be doing. With that being said, I'm going to be accepting my invitation to the arts college to do what truly lights my soul on fire."

Although this conversation created so much drama in Ethan's external world, it brought love and peace to him internally by knowing that he had put himself first.

Everyone has a 'Bruce' in their life. Someone or something (religion, society, family) who projects their own expectations and needs (Values) on to others. Once you understand how important recognising this is for your own fulfilment and happiness in life, you will understand why this is the very first piece of *The Inspired Life Method*. With that in mind, let's determine your Values.

Values Determination Process

We are about to determine your Values. But before we can, you need to understand what real Values are and not what most people mistakenly think. Values are the biggest foundational piece to living a fulfilled life. This will be the biggest chapter. Take a sip of coffee and focus closely.

What Are Values?

Your Values are your *life priorities.* They are the **areas of life** that are most intrinsically important, valuable and fulfilling to you. They come from your *perceived voids* throughout your life. (I'll explain this soon.) We all have our own unique set of Values that are as unique as our fingerprints. NO-ONE has the exact same Values as anyone else. Values

18

are areas of your life that you *do*. If you can't physically *do* a Value, it is not a Value. It is probably a social expectation you've adopted believing what you should Value.

(Hot tip: Reread that paragraph a couple of times and don't worry. I will explain it in more detail and give heaps of examples.)

What Values Are Not

Values are not social expectations, feelings, emotions or character traits.

These are NOT Values:

- Freedom.

- Honesty.

- Loyalty.

- Respect.

- Integrity.

- Control.

Let's play a little game. Pretend that you THINK you Value freedom. Pretend I transfer a billion dollars into your bank account right now. You now have ultimate time and financial freedom.

Would you just go sit on your couch and watch Netflix and do nothing else for the rest of your life? Absolutely not. You would do the things you actually Value. If you Value your family, you'd spend more time with them and do more things for them. If you Value experiences, you might travel around the world. If you Value your health, you'd get the best trainer and supplements on the market. If you Value business, you'd continue to build your business. If you Value wealth, you'd buy assets. If you Value image, you'd maybe go buy a beautiful home and maybe even some cosmetic work done. If you Value learning, you'd sign up to the best mentors and masterminds you could find.

You don't Value freedom. Freedom allows you to live out your Values. See the difference?

Let's use honesty as another example. (This is a lot funnier when you do it with a crowd.) Right now, if you see yourself as someone who 'Values' honesty, or you see yourself as an honest person, raise your hand, yes, literally put your hand in the air. Now keep your hand in the air if you've told a lie at any time in your life.

(The crowd always laughs at that moment.)

Why? The fact is we all demonstrate all character traits. I've lied before, I've also been honest; I've been mean before, but I've also been nice; I've been selfish before, yet I've also been selfless. Character traits are not Values. Now, don't get me wrong – can you have a preference for certain traits over others? Of course you can. You probably prefer someone being honest more than dishonest. That's fine, but honesty isn't a Value.

Some people will be triggered hearing this, that's okay as well. Think of Values as areas of life that you can live out and express. If you can't live out that Value by spending money on it, spending time thinking about it, spending time doing it, building a career/business expressing it or spending time talking about it, then it's probably an emotion or character trait rather than a Value. Also, you may be being too specific, instead of saying you Value honesty, maybe you Value communication. Again, you'll understand this more once you've gone through the process.

Guilt and low self-worth are feedback letting someone know they are not prioritising their own Values, but are putting someone else's Values ahead of their own.

READ THAT LINE AGAIN.

If you're feeling really down, negative, beating yourself up and struggling with your self-esteem/confidence, I guarantee that you are not prioritising your own Values. We'll do a quick exercise to

20

demonstrate this at the end of this chapter and I'll share Liv's case study to give you a real example.

Projecting Values

Whenever you hear someone using any of the following phrases, someone is projecting their Values onto someone else:

- Have to.
- Ought to.
- Should.
- Must.
- Got to.
- Need to.
- Supposed to.

(Hot tip: when someone uses any of those phrases, ask the question - According to who? The answer will be: According to whoever is projecting their Values.)

I'm going to share some examples that may trigger you, if you have a similarly high Value of the people in the examples. Let's do it.

Example 1:

Sarah is a loving mother, whose highest Value is <u>Family</u>. She works out at the gym two to three times a week and has reasonably good health. She has a friend, Julie, who is a bodybuilder and whose highest Value is <u>Health</u>. Julie says to Sarah, "You <u>need</u> to go to the gym more and you <u>should</u> sign up for this bodybuilding competition." Sarah decides to listen to Julie, even though she authentically doesn't want to. Sarah now trains every day, sometimes twice a day. She also now experiences **guilt** and **low self-worth** because she isn't spending enough time with her <u>family</u>, because she allowed Julie to project her Values on to her.

Example 2:

Geoff is a motivated business owner whose highest Value is <u>Business</u>. Geoff works every day to build his business, only stopping to rest when he physically needs to recharge. Geoff's mother, Lisa, has a high Value on <u>family</u>, and thinks he doesn't spend enough time with his family. Lisa tells Geoff, "You <u>should</u> spend more time with your family. Family is the most important thing in the world." Because Geoff doesn't understand his own Values and he doesn't have firm boundaries, he listens to his mother. Geoff starts to cut back hours on his <u>business</u> to spend time with his <u>family</u>. His <u>business</u> starts to decline, he has **guilt, low self-worth** and also resentment towards his mother, because he isn't living his own Values. He is living to his mother's.

Example 3:

Michelle is a very beautiful model whose highest Value is <u>Image</u>. She loves to look after herself by getting her hair done, her nails done, skin appointments and having nice clothes. Beccy is an insecure woman who follows Michelle online and who doesn't have a high Value on <u>image</u>. Beccy sees that Michelle always shows off her looks on social media, which annoys her. Beccy decides to message Michelle saying, "You <u>need</u> to stop showing yourself off on social media. You're just seeking attention." Michelle understands that Beccy is just projecting her Values onto her, so she decides to ignore the message and keeps prioritising her Values. Be like Michelle.

Disclaimer: The lesson from these examples is to recognise when someone is projecting their Values on to you. However, I'm not saying never to consider anyone's feedback, there can be truth in what they are saying. You'll learn to distinguish between someone projecting their Values on to you versus someone giving you practical feedback from which you can benefit. Let's continue.

Here are the signs of when you are living to your higher Values versus when you are living to your lower Values:

High Value Signs:

- **Adaptability**: When things go wrong or problems arise, you'll be willing to adapt and keep moving forward within your Values.

- **Resilience**: You'll be willing to push through pain and challenges because your Values are meaningful to you.

- **Mission driving (long-term thinking)**: You think long-term within your Values, and don't just look for quick fixes.

- **Attention**: You have higher levels of attention when you're 'doing' your Values. Have you noticed that within conversations when the topic changes to something you're interested in (a high Value of yours) you pay more attention?

- **Identification**: Whatever your highest Values are will be the way you identify yourself. If you have a high Value on business, you'll call yourself an entrepreneur. If you have a high Value on family or parenting, you'll call yourself a mother or a father. If you have a high Value on coaching, you'll call yourself a coach.

- **Reliability**: You'll be reliable within your high Values. People can depend on you to follow through with your high Values.

- **Inspired from within (intrinsic)**: *The need for motivation is a symptom of an uninspired goal.* You don't need external motivation to do your Values. You might say you're not a motivated person, I say bullshit to that. You're simply not motivated to do things that are low Values to you. However, you're 'motivated' (inspired) to do the things that are high Values for you. A parent with a high Value on family doesn't need motivation to spend time with their children. An entrepreneur with a high Value on business doesn't need motivation to work on their business. An explorer with a high Value on experiences doesn't need motivation to travel the world.

- **Certainty**: You will have higher levels of certainty when you are *doing* your high Values.

- **Discipline**: You will have more discipline with your higher Values. That's because you're doing the things that you're intrinsically driven to do. Roger Federer was disciplined when it came to tennis, but if someone *forced* him to do something that he didn't Value, he wouldn't have the same level of discipline to do that.

Are you starting to get it?

Low Value Signs:

- **Procrastination**: You will procrastinate over things for which you have a low Value. I procrastinate about cleaning because I don't Value cleaning very highly.

- **Extrinsically motivated**: You require extrinsic motivation to do things. Think of getting a child to clean their room – at some stage a child will often receive extrinsic motivation to clean the room, such as money, time on their phone/video games, or being allowed to see their friends. Why does the child require extrinsic motivation? Because the child has a low Value on cleaning the room.

(Hot tip: Get the child to see how cleaning the room will benefit their Values. We will be doing this tool later on.)

- **Poor Attention (ADHD)**: I could talk for hours on this point, but I'll keep it short. I was diagnosed with Asperger's, autism and ADHD, so this is just my personal view on this topic. Someone with ADHD is someone who has a high level of energy and high sensitivity to boredom. Because life is always balanced, if you have <u>Attention Deficit</u> somewhere, you will have <u>Attention Surplus</u> somewhere else. So, if you get someone with ADHD to do something that is boring them (a low Value to them) they will get bored and become easily distracted. However, if you get that same person to do something they are interested in (a high Value to them) they will be hyper-focused on it for extended periods. I struggled to focus in geography class (I didn't Value geography), but I could play video games (I Valued video games) for six hours straight without getting distracted. *You will have poor levels of attention when it comes to things you don't Value.*

- **Poor Retention (learning difficulty)**: You will retain less information about anything that falls within your lower Values.

- **Immediate Gratification**: You will seek immediate gratification when you are doing things that are low on your Values.

I'm sure you can see the power of knowing what your Values are and being able to structure your life around them. I'll give you just a little bit more context and then we will determine your Values.

Where Do Values Come From?

As I mentioned before, your Values come from your **perceived voids**. Whatever was a void (painful) for you, becomes important for you later. You essentially go through life 'filling your own voids'. Let's use some examples:

- You had a void (pain) around money growing up. Your parents had fights over money, they may have split up over money or you didn't have money for the things you wanted. Chances are, you now have a high Value on money or wealth.

- You had a void (pain) around your image growing up. You were the uglier sibling, family members commented on your weight, and you were bullied for the way that you looked. Chances are, you now have a high Value on image or appearance.

- You had a void (pain) around <u>family</u> growing up. Your family life was painful or wasn't the way you wanted it to be. Maybe a parent was absent, or there was abuse within the household, or maybe your needs weren't met by your parents. Chances are, you now have a high Value on family or parenting.

- You had a void (pain) around <u>health</u> growing up. You were overweight, you got bullied for your weight, maybe you had health problems, maybe you had injuries or maybe you constantly had to have medical help. Chances are, you now have a high Value on health or wellness.

- You had a void (pain) around <u>relationships</u> growing up. Your parents had a very unhealthy relationship, maybe you had unhealthy relationships when you were younger or maybe you even got cheated on. Chances are, you now have a high Value on relationships.

- You had a void (pain) around <u>learning</u> growing up. You struggled at school, maybe you were put into 'special' learning classes, maybe your parents were really hard on you with your learning and if you got a 99/100, you were made to feel stupid. Chances are, you now have a high Value on learning or growth.

This is where the famous quote, *"The greater the pain, greater the purpose,"* becomes real. Your greatest pains (voids) become your greatest strengths. I wouldn't be the man I'm proud to be, with all of my strengths, if it weren't for all of the pain I experienced in my upbringing.

Here's a list of common Values that I've found with clients. Keep in mind, there are endless amounts, and each person may use different words to describe the same thing:

- Family
- Health/wellness
- Money/wealth
- Career

- Business
- Education/learning/self-growth
- Adventure/experiences
- Spirituality
- Community
- Communication
- Leadership
- Travel
- Dancing
- Music
- Nature
- Animals
- Relationships
- Friendships
- Sensuality/sexuality
- Image
- Beauty
- Home
- Pleasure
- Entertainment
- Art
- Teaching
- Coaching
- Games
- Food

We've covered a lot about what Values are, what they aren't, what the signs of them are and where Values come from. The time has come to do the Values Determination Process...

How to Do the Process

Rules to follow:

- Answer all questions. There are 16 total questions, (though three are clarifying questions).

- Use no more than one or two words for your answers.

- Be objective and brutally honest. Don't use answers that you *should* or *have to* put down. Pretend a drone followed you around all day. What would the objective answers be from the drone?

- It is normal to have a lot of the same or similar answers for many questions. The last time I did my Values, 'Coaching' was the answer for 11 of the 13 questions.

- They must be areas of life that you can 'do'. Don't use character traits, feelings, emotions or societal expectations.

- The Values will come from voids. Ask yourself once you've determined them, 'Were these voids (painful) for me?'

- The extra three questions will be worded as part 1 and part 2 of the same question. Use part 2 as the Value for that question.

The steps you will take:

1. Answer all questions.

2. Categorise all the same or similar answers together and decide on the label or title of that Value.

3. List your Values in order from most important – the Value that showed up most often in your answers – to the least important.

4. Congratulate yourself on determining your Values.

I have included an online version of this exercise with free video training if you prefer to use technology or videos for learning. Go to www.lewishuckstep.com/book or scan the QR code below.

If you'd like to see an example of a completed table, skip to page 32 to see my example of my most recent Values Determination.

Step 1: Answer all questions in the table provided on page 35. (remember use only one or two words per answer). I recommend using a pencil, because you will do this exercise more than once:

1. <u>What do you currently spend the most time doing?</u>

    Consider all 168 hours in your average week, excluding time sleeping.

2. **Part 1:** <u>What item, object or person do you most constantly have in your personal space?</u>

    What makes you feel 'naked' when you forget or misplace it?

    Part 2: <u>Why do you constantly have that in your personal space?</u>

    What is its dominant use? What does it represent? - (Use this answer for step 2).

3. <u>What activity lights you up most and stimulates energy and enthusiasm?</u>

    What do you do for hours on end without being mentally drained or burning out? What do you do that makes you lose track of time?

4. **Part 1:** <u>Where does most of your money go each month?</u>

    What are your greatest expenses? Include investments. Be objective. Look at your bank accounts and sort your expenses by greatest to least.

Part 2: <u>Why do you spend your money on that?</u>

What does it represent for you? - (Use this answer for step 2).

5. <u>What do you focus on and think about most that's now manifesting in your life?</u>

Don't include negative self-talk, fears and worries.

6. **Part 1**: <u>Who do you admire most in life?</u>

Who are your heroes? Who do you look up to most?

Part 2: <u>What area of their life do you admire the most?</u> - (Use this answer for step 2).

7. <u>In what area of life do you receive the greatest 'income' or 'reward' from the world around you?</u>

For example:

-   Recognition for your physical beauty or performance.

-   Financial income.

-   Insights from studying great minds.

-   Positive feedback from your clients.

-   Reward of seeing your children thriving.

-   Praise from your followers and community.

-   Unconditional love from god/universe.

8. <u>What do you talk about most?</u>

What topic do you automatically pull your conversations towards? What topic of conversation lights you up most?

9. <u>What do you read, watch and learn about most?</u>

When you walk into a bookstore, what section are you most drawn to? What's common about the books, courses, masterminds and mentorship programs you buy? What do you watch or listen to most on YouTube and podcasts? What are you constantly Googling, researching and studying most?

10. <u>Where do you have the most order and organisation in your life?</u>

Where do you have the most routine, structure and systems? What areas do you measure and analyse most diligently?

11. <u>In what area of life do you have the most ambition, persistence and resilience?</u>

Ambition is your willingness to embrace the good and bad, happy and sad, ups and downs, positives and negatives. Don't include areas where you constantly give up, quit or change direction.

12. <u>What do you set goals for most that actually shows evidence of coming true?</u>

Don't include fantasies that have no evidence of coming true.

13. <u>What inspires you most?</u>

What gives you awe-inspired goose bumps or tears of inspiration? Where do you lose track of time or get in 'the zone'?

On the next page is an example of my Values Determination questions for reference.

My Answers

TABLE 1	Answer #1	Answer #2	Answer #3
1. Time: What do you currently spend the most time doing?	Coaching	Learning	Relationships
2. Space - Part 1: What item, object or person do you most constantly have in your personal space?	Phone	Books	Georgia
Clarity Space - Part 2: What's its dominant use? What does it represent?	Coaching	Learning	Relationship
3. Energy: What activity lights you up most and stimulates energy and enthusiasm?	Coaching	Learning	Training
4. Money - Part 1: Where does most of your money go each month?	Events	Health	Investments
Clarify Money - Part 2: Why do you spend your money on that? What does it represent for you?	Learning	Health	Wealth

5. Focus: What do you focus on and think about most that's now manifesting in your life?	Coaching	Wealth	Relationship
6. Admiration - Part 1: Who do you admire most in life?	Dr John Demartini	Tony Robbins	Peter Crone
Clarify Admiration - Part 2: What area of their life do you admire most?	Learning	Relationship	Coaching
7. Income: In what area of life do you receive the greatest 'income' or 'reward' from the world around you?	Coaching	Relationship	Health
8. Conversation: What do you talk about most?	Self-development / learning	Relationships	Wealth
9. Learning: What do you read, watch and learn about most?	Coaching	Wealth	Relationships

10. Order: Where do you have the most order and organisation in your life?	Coaching	Wealth	Relationships
11. Ambition: In what area of life do you have the most ambition, persistence and resilience?	Coaching	Learning	Relationships
12. Goals: What do you set goals for most, that actually show evidence of coming true?	Coaching	Wealth	Learning
13. Inspiration: What inspires you most?	Coaching	Relationships	Learning

Use your answers from the previous questions and put them into this table:

TABLE 2	Answer #1	Answer #2	Answer #3
1. Time: What do you currently spend the most time doing?			
2. Space - Part 1: What item, object or person do you most constantly have in your personal space?			
Clarity Space - Part 2: What's its dominant use? What does it represent?			
3. Energy: What activity lights you up most and stimulates energy and enthusiasm?			
4. Money Part 1: Where does most of your money go each month?			
Clarify Money - Part 2: Why do you spend your money on that? What does it represent for you?			

5. Focus: What do you focus on and think about most that's now manifesting in your life?			
6. Admiration – **Part 1:** Who do you admire most in life?			
Clarify Admiration - **Part 2:** What area of their life do you admire most?			
7. Income: In what area of life do you receive the greatest 'income' or 'reward' from the world around you?			
8. Conversation: What do you talk about most?			
9. Learning: What do you read, watch and learn about most?			
10. Order: Where do you have the most order and organisation in your life?			

11. Ambition: In what area of life do you have the most ambition, persistence and resilience?			
12. Goals: What goals do you set most for which there is evidence they actually could come true?			
13. Inspiration: What inspires you most?			

Step 2: Categorise all the same or similar answers together. Decide on the label or title of that Value. (Remember to only use Part 2 of the clarifying questions.) Using my example in Table 1 you can see my answers are very similar and refined. That's because I've done this process more than thirty times. The more you do this, the clearer and more refined you will become. However, you can see I have the answers 'Training' and 'Health'. I personally would categorise this as health, but you might use a different word like wellness, and that's perfect. I also categorise 'Relationship' (intimate relationship) in the same category as 'Relationships' (friendships and family). You may have these as separate Values or as the same, that's up to you. So go back to Table 2 and change the similar answers into the title of the Value that resonates most with you.

Step 3: List your Values in order from most important (the Value that showed up the most in the 13 questions) to least important (the Value that showed up the least in the 13 questions).

To use my answers from Table 1 again, here are my Values with the number of 'votes' each Value received:

1. Coaching (11)

2. Relationships (10)

3. Learning (9)

4. Wealth (6)

5. Health (3)

Tally up your answers and write your Values out in order of most votes received to least votes received. (Remember to answer only Part 1 of the 13 questions.) Ideally, you'll end up with 4–7 Values.

1.

2.

3.

4.

5.

6.

7.

Step 4: Congratulations! You've just determined your Values!!! (Fist pump into the air!) Please go to page 267 and write your Values into the section provided.

Now what do you do with them? Great question.

Remember, these tell you what's intrinsically important to you. If you don't prioritise these Values, you will experience low self-worth and guilt as feedback. So, this is what to do with your Values:

1. **Schedule your Values into your Calendar.** What doesn't get scheduled, doesn't get done. If you've ever heard about setting healthy boundaries for yourself, this is literally doing that. If you don't respect these boundaries for yourself, you will be putting other people's Values ahead of your own and therefore not

filling your own cup, and you must fill your own cup so you can be your best self for others.

2. **Stop doing things that aren't in your Values and aren't something that you want to be doing**. Sounds so simple but so many people do things because they think they 'have to, ought to, should or must'. But guess what – you don't have to.

3. **Delegate things you don't want to do but 'need' to get done, to move towards your goals**. Example: if you don't enjoy doing your bookkeeping for your business, pay someone else to do it for you. The goal is to do only what you want to do and to delegate the rest (pretty much the concept of this whole book).

4. **Link benefits: If you want something to get done but you don't want to do it yourself and you can't delegate it** – you don't have the finances to delegate or you can't physically delegate something (like training) – **you link benefits to your top three Values**. You'll learn about this in Chapter 8.

Here's the quick little exercise I referred to earlier. Quickly read over your Values. Now, pretend you weren't prioritising any of your Values and they were all going backwards in life. How would you feel? You'd probably feel down, feel guilty, lack self-worth and beat yourself up, right? Remember the line: Guilt and low self-worth is feedback to let someone know they are not prioritising their own Values but are putting someone else's Values ahead of their own. So, make sure you're putting your own oxygen mask on first. Be selfish so you can be selfless.

Yes, there are times where you will put other people's needs (Values) ahead of your own. Like having children and being in some relationships. But at least 80% of the time, do your best to prioritise your own Values.

This is the biggest chapter of this book. Well done for smashing through it! You're now clear on your Values and what to do with them. However, this is not a 'do it once and you're done for life'. This is something you need to do regularly. I've been doing my Values for eight years now. Here is my recommendation on how frequently to redo your Values:

Once a week for the first month.

Once a month for the first six months after that.

Every three months forever.

Your Values do change over time. This is why it's important to regularly check back in with yourself, to realign with who you authentically are.

Let me show you a little case study of how Values are so powerful when used in your day-to-day life:

Liv was one of my first clients who worked with me many moons ago. A young, motivated woman, she came to me to work on her mindset, to be happier and to help start her own coaching business.

We jumped on our weekly call, and I asked my usual check-in questions: "How are you personally out of 10 and how are you professionally out of 10? You can't use the number seven for these questions." Her answer was a four for both. That's not good, so I asked her, "Why are you only a four out of 10?" She responded, "I don't know, I just feel really off. I feel unmotivated, I'm doubting myself and feel really down." Interesting.

We had already determined her Values by this stage (it's the first thing I do with all of my clients), so I asked, "How did you go with prioritising your Values this week?" Her face instantly changed; I could see her realisation of where I was about to take our conversation. I continued with, "Let's go through your top three Values (which were health, business and friendships). How did you go with your health this week?" Her response, "Terrible, I haven't trained at all this week, and I've eaten poorly." There was the first clue. "What about your second Value of business. How did you go with working on your business this week?" I asked. "Terrible," she said again, "I haven't done any work on my business." Interesting, I thought. "What about your third Value – how'd you go with your friendships this week?" Can you guess her answer? "Not good. I haven't caught up with any of my friends this week."

Straightaway, I got Liv to open up her calendar and schedule in her Values. I also got her to commit to prioritising herself until I saw her the following week. The results were exactly what you're expecting.

The next week I was greeted by a very different Liv. This Liv was full of energy, felt inspired and answered 10/10 for both the check-in questions. "What's changed since last week?" I asked, already knowing the answer. Liv responded, "I know it sounds so simple, but I actually just lived my Values. I prioritised my health, friendships and business. I feel incredible and I feel inspired." How good is that?

This may seem like such an obvious solution now that you understand Values, but most people make those same mistakes every day.

If you want to see Liv's video testimonial just scan the QR code below or go to this link: https://youtu.be/Pzewcb0bfc0

I'm sure you now see the power of what knowing and prioritising their Values can do for someone and for the fulfilment of their life. As Dr John Demartini puts it: "*If you live life based on your lower Values, you will be a victim of your history. If you live a life based on your highest Values, you will be the master of your destiny.*"[2]

2 "What Is the Purpose of Life? - Discover Your Purpose on Earth I Dr John

This is just the first step of *The Inspired Life Method*. There are a lot more pieces to put in place, and all the pieces build on each other.

Figure 4

Values done✓

Summary of Values:

1. Your Values are what intrinsically fulfil you.

2. Low self-worth is feedback that you're not prioritising your Values.

3. Redo your Values at least every three months because your Values do change over time.

Here's a deep question: What's your life's Purpose? Many people struggle to answer this. What if I told you there's a step-by-step process to discovering yours? It's in the next chapter so let's get into it.

Demartini," YouTube video, 12:34, posted by Dr John Demartini, August 22, 2024, https://www.youtube.com/watch?v=qOTzcbBB42Y&ab_channel=DrJohnDemartini.

CHAPTER 3

Your Calling:

Finding Your Life's Purpose

"Your Purpose in life is to find your Purpose..."
– Gautama Buddha

"What the fuck is going on with you?" my partner asked me, as tears were streaming down my face...

I sit down and sink into the couch with Georgia after another long, stressful day of trying to achieve goals to prove my self-worth. We've got our favourite meal of steak, potatoes, gravy and veggies, and I also have my additional serving of avocado. (I'm an avocado addict and I'm proud of it.)

We exchange the cliché questions, "How was your day?" and "What was the highlight of your day?" But because we're both quite drained from a full day of prioritising other people's Values and not our own, we opt to watch some TV to take our minds off things.

I turn the TV on and we agree on *Shark Tank*, the US version. We both love the show because it hits some of our highest Values. If you don't know, in the show aspiring business owners pitch their business to five successful entrepreneurs (the 'Sharks'), in the hope of getting a 'deal' or investment from one or more of them. (The success rate for deals going through is about 56% over the show's history.)

Some of the pitches are laughable and we have often asked ourselves, *How did this person even make it this far?* However, there have also been some very inspiring success stories. Some of the pitches result in deals that make the Shark and the business owner many millions of dollars, sometimes even more than $100 million. It genuinely changes people's lives, which is why I really enjoy the show.

The episode that evening starts with a 15-year-old boy, Trey Brown, walking in with his mum. They're in the clothing industry, with their business called Spergo. Trey starts off the pitch, saying, "I'm powerful, I'm strong, I'm courageous and we have an impact that's changing the world." He then starts to share the ins and outs of their business – who they are, why they started, what they stand for, what their Vision is for the future and what they are offering the Sharks (what percentage of their business they're offering to sell and for how much). In this case, Trey was asking for $300,000 in exchange for 10% of Spergo. Instantly all the Sharks are impressed with his energy and the passion he has for his business.

After the initial introduction, the Sharks then start asking about the business and the people involved. (They need to feel confident that, if they decide to invest in the business, they will get a return on their investment.) One of the obvious questions that gets asked every time is, "What's the revenue or total sales of the business?" The Sharks were blown away when Trey told them, "To this day, our total sales are $1.8 million dollars." Not bad for a 15-year-old, right?

The Sharks continued by asking where Trey wanted to take the business. Throughout the pitches, the Sharks either choose not to invest by saying, "I'm out" or they make an offer to buy into the business being pitched, by matching what the business owner wants or making a counteroffer. Three Sharks pulled out of the deal because their expertise in business was not a strong match for Spergo, and the two remaining Sharks were Mark Cuban and Daymond John.

Cuban had great success in online broadcasting, and sold his company, Broadcast.com, for $5.7 billion in 1997. He also owns a sizable percentage (27%) of the Dallas Mavericks NBA team. John is well known as the clothing Shark, who's had success in that industry with his company, FUBU. Of the two, he was the obvious match for Trey, but either Shark had yet to make an offer.

Throughout Trey's entire pitch, Cuban had been very encouraging and supportive, clapping and fist pumping as he chanted, "Yeah, Trey, that's what's up!" and many other supportive comments. I kept feeling a wave of emotions move through me – I was even teary. After the three other Sharks had dropped out of the deal, it was time for Mark to weigh in: "The Vision is great, but you have to walk to the Vision, not run. Because you want to see what's right in front of you and all around you." He continued, "Now I don't do clothes, but I do help young superstars. And I do want to enable people with dreams to accomplish things that some other people might not think is possible. And so, I'll offer you $300,000 for 25% of the company."

By this time tears are running down my face. My partner looks at me and asks, "What the fuck's going on with you?" This story wasn't the most tear-jerking story from *Shark Tank*, not by a long shot, but something I was seeing was giving me tears of inspiration. A mentor had once told me, "When you get tears of inspiration, you are seeing or doing something that's aligned with your Purpose." I also knew by this time that our Purpose in life is an expression of our biggest core wound (once we've healed through it). So, I ask myself: *What is it specifically about this episode that's giving me these tears of inspiration?*

It hit me. The mentorship/guidance/coaching that Mark Cuban was giving young Trey, was what I didn't receive from my dad. And right then I really felt it. I also knew that we become who we needed when we were at our lowest. All the moments when we're feeling inspired, especially when we get the tears of inspiration, are all breadcrumbs from the Universe revealing our Purpose and our Values. Please be aware of all of those moments as you move forwards in your life.

In the end, Trey accepted the offer from John, and the company is still very successful to this day.

If you'd like to watch the full episode just search on YouTube for Shark Tank Spergo or use the link:

https://youtu.be/tXYV-b4Q1a8?si=Fr6rnamkX6Ddg7AW

The Purpose Process

"When what you do is the fullest expression of who you are, you will do your life's best work."

– Lewis Huckstep

Many people ask themselves, *What's my Purpose in life?* And no, you don't have to meditate in the mountains or take plant medicine for years to answer that question. Once you understand what a Purpose is, and you complete the Purpose Process in this chapter, you will know what your Purpose is and how to use it. I know that is a big claim, that's why I'm excited to bring it to you.

What Is a Purpose?

There are many definitions for what a Purpose is. My definition is:

"Your Purpose is your gift to give back to the world."

Your Purpose is your greatest gift that you can give back to others. It is the driving force that inspires you more than anything else. It is both your Guiding Star offering you direction for where you want to go in life and the unlimited fuel source that allows you to pursue your Purpose and fulfil your Mission.

Where Does Your Purpose Come From?

Again, many people have different answers to this question. Some people believe that no one has a Purpose other than to exist, while others believe that you are born with your 'Soul's Purpose' and life will reveal that to you.

My answer is, "<u>Your Purpose is an expression of your biggest core wound</u>" – once you've healed the wound. Until you heal the wound, it will continue to be a trigger for you. (We discuss this and do healing work in Chapter 9.) If you've ever heard of the quote "*Turn pain into Purpose*" or "*Turn your wounds into wisdom*", this is what that means.

Essentially, whatever was most painful for you (your biggest wound), will give you the most Purpose. This ties into Values (remember, voids become Values), and that's why we do Values first. But to really hit the nail on the head, you need to identify your greatest core wound, and we're about to do exactly that.

Before we do, here are some examples of what a core wound, expressed as a Purpose, could be:

1. **Core wound:** Feeling/being unloved and not wanted.

   Purpose: Helping others find love within themselves and build fulfilling relationships.

2. **Core wound:** Suppressing true self-expression to fit into societal, familial or religious expectations.

   Purpose: Encouraging authenticity and helping individuals embrace their true selves.

3. **Core wound:** Feeling the need to be flawless to be accepted.

   Purpose: Helping others embrace their imperfections and authenticity.

4. **Core wound:** Feeling victimised by those in authority.

   Purpose: Empowering others to stand against abuse and promoting leadership with integrity.

My core wound: Feeling unsafe, hurt and rejected.

My Purpose: To heal and expand consciousness.

My wounds around feeling unsafe and hurt due to the physical, mental and emotional abuse of my upbringing have gifted me my Purpose to heal others. The pain of feeling rejected by friends, family and any social group for being weird (being diagnosed with Asperger's and ADHD added to this), gifted me my Purpose to expand other people's consciousness. My greatest wounds are my greatest gifts.

I'm sure you're starting to see the power of this. However, enough about me – it's your turn to discover your Purpose.

Tips for doing the Purpose Process:

- Make sure you're in a really calm, neutral state. I'd suggest even doing some grounding (calming your nervous system) before doing the process. Leaning into your greatest core wound can bring up a high level of emotions, and because of this we have the next tip. I've created a breathwork and emotional regulating exercise you can use. Go to www.lewishuckstep.com/book to use it. (We'll be using this again later for the Inner Work sections.)

- Stop if the process becomes too much. Just like any form of Inner Healing work, whenever you hit a breaking point and it becomes too much, STOP. Take a breath. Come back to it later.

- Spend time on the questions and do this process many times. Your Ego (we go into detail about this in Chapter 9) wants to avoid pain, so sometimes it can be hard to answer these questions. That's where meditating and journaling on these questions can help move you through the resistance.

- Don't use words to impress others. Sometimes the simpler they are, the better.

- Your Purpose DOES NOT need to have anything to do with a business or career. It can be something like 'raising a healthy, loving family', because your core wound is around the emotionally, unsafe family upbringing you had.

- Even if you didn't have your parents in your life, still answer the questions with what comes up intuitively.

- The Extended Purpose is there to get as much out of you as you can – like brain dumping. The Refined Purpose is the refined version of your Extended Purpose.

- This is an intuitive process. Don't overthink the answers. Centre yourself, take a deep in-breath before answering each question.

Ready to rock? Let's begin...

The process:

1. Answer the first four questions, using only a one-word answer for each question.

2. Using those four words, find the theme that those words mean to you.

3. Insert the word from Step Two into the next question where instructed. Then answer the remaining questions.

4. Write out your extended Purpose statement.

5. Write out your refined Purpose statement.

I have provided examples of these questions being answered on page 54 if that helps you with the process.

Step 1: Answer the following four questions. Refine your answers for each question down to 1 or 2 words: (Remember to take a breath in before answering each question.)

1. What did you get from your mother that you didn't want?

_____

_____

2. What did you get from your father that you didn't want?

_____

_____

3. What did you want from your mother that you didn't get?

_____

_____

4. What did you want from your father that you didn't get?

_____

_____

Step 2: Using all four answers from the previous questions, what is the theme that you can see/feel? Use one word to answer this question.

_____

Step 3: Use your answer from Step 2 and insert that word in the space at the end of the following question. Use as many words as you need for these questions. Aim for a couple of sentences.

1. What is your biggest core wound around feeling/being _____ ?

_____

_____

2. What is a real-life example of you experiencing this core wound (your previous answer)? Really feel the emotions of this answer but stop if you need to.

_____

_____

3. How old were you when you experienced this core wound?

_____

_____

4. What did you need back then?

_____

_____

5. How can you express this core wound and give back to others?

_____

_____

Step 4: Use all your answers from Step 3, especially question 5, to write out your extended Purpose.

My Purpose is ...

_____

Step 5: Look at your answer from Step 4. Find the core meaning of that answer. Refine that answer down into 1 to 2 sentences.

My Purpose is...

_____

_____

_____

_____

My example of The Purpose Process:

Step 1: Answer the following four questions. Refine your answers for each question down to 1 to 2 words: (Remember to take a breath in before answering each question.)

1. What did you get from your mother that you didn't want? *Weakness*

2. What did you get from your father that you didn't want? *Hurt*

3. What did you want from your mother that you didn't get? *Strength*

4. What did you want from your father that you didn't get? *Safety*

Step 2: Using all four answers from the previous questions, what is the theme that you can see/feel? Use one word to answer this question.

Unsafe

Step 3: Use your answer from Step 2 and insert that word into the following question where instructed. Use as many words as you need for these questions. Aim for a couple of sentences.

1. What is your biggest core wound around feeling/being *unsafe*?

   Feeling unsafe around my dad and others. To express myself. To regulate my emotions. To be my true self.

2. What is a real-life example of you experiencing this core wound? Really feel the emotions of this answer but stop if you need to.

   Sitting at the dinner table and feeling anxious, scared and fearful of my Dad. Being scared of Dad snapping with anger towards me or my family.

3. How old were you when you experienced this core wound? *7*

4. What did you need back then?

   Help healing. To regulate my emotions. To know I was safe. To be seen. To be loved. To know how to express myself.

5. How can you express this core wound and give back to others?

To help others heal. To help them feel safe. To teach them how to express their true selves. To help them regulate their emotions.

Step 4: Use all your answers from Step 3, especially question five, to write out your extended Purpose.

My Purpose is ...

To help others heal through their wounds, pains, traumas and limitations. To help others feel safe to express their true selves and know that they are enough.

Step 5: Look at your answer from Step 4. Find the core meaning of that answer. Refine that answer down into 1 to 2 sentences.

My Purpose is ...

To heal and expand consciousness.

Congratulations! You've just discovered your Purpose. If this is your first time doing this level of self-development or self-exploration, you may have experienced a lot of resistance during that process. That's okay. That's why we redo the process. Just like Values, you redo this process regularly.

Take a moment to look at your Purpose. Say it out loud. How does that sound? If you don't feel a level of energy within you, you're not clear enough yet. That's okay. Come back and redo this process in the near future. If you did feel emotions throughout that process, especially for Step 3, imagine focusing those emotions and energy towards your life's goals (Mission). Pretty powerful, right? When I read over my Purpose statement, I don't need motivation. The energy that it brings up inspires me to do the work that needs to get done to achieve my Mission.

Go to page 266 and add your Purpose into the section provided.

Now you might be wondering: *What do I do with my Purpose? How do I use it?* Great questions. Here are the answers:

1. It's your unlimited fuel source. Have it somewhere you can see it (phone background, on your mirror, on the fridge) and read it daily.

2. Create a life where you get to express your Purpose at the highest level. Remember the quote, *"When what you do is the fullest expression of who you are, you will do your life's best work"* Don't worry, this book will show you how to do exactly that.

3. Set a Mission that is aligned with your Purpose. We're about to do that in the next chapter.

4. Continue to refine your Purpose. Meditation, plant medicine and journaling can help massively with this.

Let me show you the power of what being clear on your Purpose can do for you. Here is a true story about a good friend of mine:

Dion and I have known each other for more than seven years and have always supported each other in life and business, even though we live in different cities. Dion is a very energetic character who has always taken action towards his goals, opening up multiple businesses in many industries. He was moderately successful with some but others failed. He bounced between different business opportunities that he wasn't truly inspired by, but he was fired up about life and taking action, like a bull in a china shop.

We caught up in person after the COVID lockdowns ended, and we hadn't seen each other for about two years. I asked the obvious question, "How have things been?" He responded, "Man, I've honestly started like five different things and haven't finished any of them."

In my coaching mind this was a huge sign that he was either not clear on his Purpose, or those five different things weren't in alignment with his Purpose.

So, I asked him, "What's your Purpose?" His answer was, "To unlock people's infinite potential, to maximise the limitless capacity of others."

Wow, that was a lot to take in. I followed up with, "Where does your Purpose come from?" He froze. "I don't know," was his response. "I've never been asked that before."

With all the firm love in the world, I told him, "Don't take this the wrong way, but it sounds like you've just put words in your Purpose to impress others. The way I teach Purpose is that it comes from your biggest core wound." I explained what my Purpose and core wound was. He was really amazed, in fact stunned, by that conversation.

Two weeks then passed, and Dion gave me a call. "Brother, since our conversation, I've been having all of these flashbacks and very vivid dreams. I've been having these memories of really painful things about my dad and childhood." He told me he'd had flashbacks of his dad holding his head under water so he couldn't breathe, of his dad embarrassing him in front of his friends, telling him, "You'll never amount to anything." Dion said he had no previous memory of some of these things.

He continued, "I called my mum and asked her if these things happened, and she broke down into tears." She told him, "All of those are true. I wasn't going to tell you any of it unless you asked me directly about it." I responded to Dion, "That's pretty powerful. What emotions does that bring up for you?" To which he replied, "So much, man. It makes me want to run through walls to do something with it."

After another week, we spoke again on the phone, and I will never forget what he shared with me. "Brother, I think I've found my Purpose," he said with inspiration. "What is it?" I asked, curiously. "To change how people learn," he replied, with real conviction. Wow, I felt how authentic he was when he said that.

He continued, "Since our conversation I've kept thinking about what my core wound was. It kept coming up for me that I was stupid and not good enough. Honestly, changing the way people learn feels so right and aligned with who I am and where I want to go. I'm going to build a business where I teach people in a way that no one else does." Again, he had spoken with great conviction.

Now that sounds all fluffy and nice, but let's see how it actually translated into results. These conversations happened just under three years ago. Since then, Dion followed through with his Purpose-led business – helping business owners scale their business by helping them learn differently. This continuous and relentless, focused action resulted in helping his clients generate more than $73 million in under three years. Not bad at all.

Dion already had the ability and potential, like most people, but he was just lacking the right fuel source and the direction of where to go.

Figure 5

Summary of Purpose:

1. Your Purpose is your gift to give to the world.

2. It is an expression of your biggest core wound.

3. It gives you both direction of where to go and an unlimited fuel source to get there.

Bonus tip: be aware of when you get tears of inspiration. You are seeing parts of your Purpose.

Now that you know your Purpose, you've got your fuel source and you've got your direction. Now imagine knowing the clear measurable goal that you can break down into very clear actionable steps ... and also know how your life will look once you achieve it.

You're in luck. We're going to do that right now.

CHAPTER 4

Your Quest to Conquer

*"We're here to put a dent in the universe,
otherwise why else even be here?"*

– Steve Jobs

Your shiny object syndrome is what's killing your goals. You keep building unfinished bridges.

John is a mechanic but not just a normal mechanic, he's the best in his city. He loves everything to do with cars. The design. The performance. The style. The craftsmanship. Every day he goes to work, he's like a child in a candy shop. He's truly passionate about cars, and because he's so passionate, work doesn't feel like work to him. It actually brings him joy and feeds his curiosity. Once he finishes his shift he keeps researching, studying, designing and visualising cars and the potential they have. He is living very aligned with his Values and Purpose.

John had many dreams. He wanted to start his own mechanic shop. He wanted to work with professional F1 racers. He wanted to design his own cars. He wanted to work with rare vintage cars that most people never get to see. He wanted to be a professional racer himself. His list of dreams continued to get bigger and bigger. He felt like he had some sort of condition that he couldn't turn off. In fact, what John was suffering from was more common than he first thought.

After eight years and after trying 13 business ideas, John had not progressed significantly with any of his ventures. They all were exciting and fun to start, but after a few months the hype had worn off, the results plateaued, and his belief in the idea started to die. So, he had moved on to the next idea. Eight years of not really progressing much overall built up a lot of frustration. He started asking himself why he even bothered, telling himself, *I'm just not meant to be successful. I'll just stay at my job forever.*

Thankfully, a gift was on its way.

John was at a family get-together for Christmas. He decided to speak with his Uncle Alex, a very successful business owner. Alex and John had spoken many times at family gatherings, but John never sought direct advice before. Instead, he just told his uncle all the new business ideas he had and how excited he was about them. This time though, because of his frustration and feeling really down about his lack of business success, he decided to ask for some advice. The conversation would change John's life forever.

John explained his situation and all about where he was at and where he wanted to go. Then he asked, "What should I do?"

Alex's answer: "John, you suffer from a common disease that most people who are early in their business journey suffer from. The disease of shiny object syndrome. You keep building unfinished bridges. It's like you're trying to play 10 sports and be a pro at all of them within a few months, but once you realise that you haven't 'made it', you quit and go start a different sport. You keep failing against the same boss [challenge], thinking that changing the game will solve it, until you run into the same boss [challenge] again. You need to pick one Mission, commit to it and go all in it for an extremely long time. This allows you to get the compounding returns of continuous focus on a single goal. If you don't, you'll keep building unfinished bridges. Answer this question for yourself: What's the one thing that lights you up the most and you could do for the longest period of time?"

Wow! John's whole view of reality changed from that one conversation.

That night, because he couldn't stop thinking about it, he sat at his desk and mapped out all of the potential goals he could chase. He kept asking himself the question his uncle had asked, *What's the one thing that lights you up the most and you could do for the longest time?*

After weighing up all of the options that could work, John decided on one. He committed to it and went all in on his goal.

Fast forward 10 years and John had built a $30 million business. He had beaten the 'bosses' (challenges) with whom he had kept failing before the conversation with his uncle. What was so interesting and inspiring about John's journey was that seven years into pursuing this goal, his business was only worth a million dollars, but in the following three years it grew 2,900%!

You see, most people never get the compounded growth because they never finish building their bridge.

Setting Your Mission and Vision

"If you want to be happy, set a goal that commands your thoughts, liberates your energy, and inspires your hopes."
— Andrew Carnegie

Figure 6

So, you now know your Values (what fulfils you the most in life), and you know your life's Purpose (your gift to give back). It's now time to create your life's Mission and Vision. Just a reminder – we are focusing on your PERSONAL Mission and Vision, not your business Mission and Vision. Depending on what you decide to do for your business (if you start a business at all), the Mission and Vision may be the same as your personal ones or they can be different.

Firstly, let's define the two terms:

Mission: A Mission is a five to ten-year measurable goal that is derived from (and aligned with) your Purpose. It gives you a clear measurable goal that can then be broken down into very specific steps, so you can take action towards it. The term BHAG (Big Hairy Audacious Goal) is very commonly used with the term Mission.

Vision: A Vision is a very detailed description of what your life looks like, once you have achieved the Mission.

Let's start with the Mission.

<u>Why is it important to have a very clear Mission?</u>

- It gives you a clear measurable goal to break down.

- It gives you time to make mistakes, learn, grow and have compounding growth. (The graph on the next page goes into more detail about this.)

- It stops you switching from idea to idea and building unfinished bridges.

- It inspires and requires you to grow into the person who's worthy of achieving the Mission.

The Emotional Roller-Coaster of Success

Expanding on one of the previous points – having a big five to ten-year goal (Mission) gives you time to go through the emotional roller-coaster of success that every single person goes through.

62

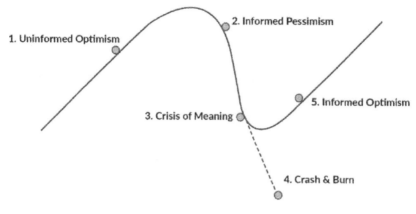

Figure 7[3]

When you start any new venture to achieve any goal, you go through each of these five stages:

1. **Uninformed Optimism:** You are uninformed about the reality of what is needed to achieve the goal and you think it will be easy.

2. **Informed Pessimism:** You start to become informed about the reality of what is needed to achieve the goal, and you start to doubt if you can achieve the goal.

3. **Crisis of Meaning (Valley of Despair):** You're confronted with big challenges (bosses) to test you and force you to either grow or to give up.

4. **Crash and Burn (Give Up):** You can't handle the challenges (bosses), so you crash and burn or just give up.

---

[3] Tim Ferriss, "Harnessing Entrepreneurial Manic-Depression: Making the Rollercoaster Work for You," *The Blog of Author Tim Ferriss,* October 3, 2008, https://tim.blog/2008/10/03/harnessing-entrepreneurial-manic-depression-making-the-rollercoaster-work-for-you/.

5. **Informed Optimism:** You've made it through the crisis of meaning and you've grown from it. Now you're informed and optimistic about achieving your goal.

Most people go from stage 1 to 4, then go back and start again at stage 1. Repeating this over and over again and never amounting to anything meaningful, just like John the mechanic. A massive benefit of setting a big five to ten-year goal, is that it gives you time to get through the 'crisis of meaning' stage and make it to the 'informed optimism' stage.

Setting a Mission is one of the simpler processes when compared to either the Values or Purpose Processes.

Rules for Creating Your Mission Statement:

- It's something that inspires you to pursue it.

- It has something clearly measurable, so it can be broken into smaller steps later.

- It's derived from your Purpose. (Read your Purpose before creating your Mission.)

- Don't use words to impress people.

- Refine the Mission to its core objective, keeping it within one or two sentences.

- It **does not** have to be something you will build a business around. It could be 'To give my family the upbringing they deserve'. Don't feel pressured to have a Mission that requires you to build a business around it.

Examples of what using your Purpose to create a Mission Statement can look like:

Example #1:

Purpose: Helping others find love within themselves and build fulfilling relationships.

Expanded Mission Statement: Develop and implement a holistic relationship education program aimed at creating self-love, healthy communication and mutual respect, reaching at least 10,000 people annually through workshops, online courses and community events. To build fulfilling relationships.

Refined Mission Statement: Empower 10,000 people to build fulfilling relationships through self-love, mutual respect and healthy communication.

Example #2:

Purpose: Assisting others in self-discovery to embrace their authentic identity.

Mission Statement: Create a retreat centre focused on personal growth and self-discovery, offering transformative workshops, holistic therapies and immersive experiences designed to help 100,000 people a year to reconnect with their authentic selves and live with Purpose and passion.

Refined Mission Statement: To help 100,000 people a year to reconnect with their authentic selves and live with Purpose and passion.

Example #3:

Purpose: Empowering women to recognise their true beauty and worth, creating confidence and self-esteem.

Mission Statement: Establish a sustainable and inclusive beauty and fashion brand for women, committed to celebrating diversity, promoting self-love and empowering individuals to embrace their unique beauty. To create a positive impact on the beauty industry by offering high-quality, cruelty-free products that cater to diverse skin tones, body types and cultural backgrounds. To launch initiatives such as confidence-building workshops, beauty mentorship programs and social media campaigns that challenge narrow beauty standards and encourage authenticity. To reach a global audience of 1 million customers whose lives are changed forever.

<u>Refined Mission Statement</u>: To have an impact on 1 million women to embrace their own worth, self-love and unique beauty.

Steps for Creating Your Mission Statement:

Step 1: Write down your Purpose

Step 2: Answer the priming questions.

Step 3: Write out your expanded Mission Statement. (Aim for a paragraph.)

Step 4: Write out your refined Mission Statement. (Aim for one or two sentences.)

I have included my own answers as an example for you on page 70

It's your turn now. Let's begin:

Step 1: What is your Purpose?

_____

_____

_____

Step 2: Priming questions: These questions are designed to get you to think bigger and expand your awareness of what is possible. Answer these with no fear or worry about how you're going to achieve it.

1. What would you love to achieve in the next 5-10 years to fulfil your Purpose?

_____

_____

_____

2. What would you achieve if you couldn't fail?

_____

_____

_____

_____

3. What goal scares you but excites you at the same time?

_____

_____

_____

_____

Step 3: Expanded Mission Statement: Write down your expanded Mission Statement. Write down everything that comes to you. (Use your answers to the priming questions to help with this.)

My expanded Mission is...

_____

_____

_____

_____

Step 4: Refined Mission Statement: Refine your expanded Mission Statement into the core of it. Keep this within 1-2 sentences.

My refined Mission is...

_____

_____

_____

_____

Example Mission questions:

Step 1: What is your Purpose?

To Heal and Expand Consciousness

Step 2: Priming questions. These questions are designed to get you to think bigger and expand your awareness of what is possible:

1. What would you love to achieve in the next 5-10 years to fulfil your Purpose?

    To help millions of people to heal their wounds, to increase their level of awareness & consciousness. To help them create a life on their terms.

2. What would you achieve if you couldn't fail?

    Write bestselling books, run in-person events with thousands of people attending, and have online programs helping millions of people per year.

3. What goal scares you but excites you at the same time?

    To help 10 million people to heal, to discover their true self and to coach them to create a life that inspires them.

Step 3: Expanded Mission Statement: Write down your expanded Mission Statement. Write down everything that comes to you. Use your answers to the priming questions to help with this.

My expanded Mission is...

To coach 10 million people to heal through their limitations and wounds. To help them find their True Authentic Self and to create a life on their terms. To write bestselling books. To have a podcast with millions of downloads. To have online programs that serve millions of people every year.

Step 4: Refined Mission Statement: Refine your expanded Mission Statement into the core of it. Keep this within one or two sentences.

My refined Mission is...

To coach 10 million people to create a life on their terms.

Congratulations! You now have your life's Mission! Go to page 266 and add in your Mission. We will use your Mission later when we get to the Master Planning section in Chapter 7.

But we're going to keep pushing. Let's create your Vision.

A quick reminder. A Vision is a very detailed description of what your life looks like, once you have achieved the Mission.

Let's start with why it's important to have a Vision:

- You have absolute clarity on what your Dream Life looks like.
- It gives you further inspiration and energy to take the action required to create your Dream Life.
- It allows you to 'manifest' what you truly want.
- It helps you get through the inevitable problems you will face while pursuing your Mission: The 'crisis of meaning' stage.

Rules for Creating Your Life's Vision:

- It is what your life looks like once you achieve the Mission you just created, so make sure you read over your Mission again before creating your Vision.
- It is a detailed expanded version of your Values, so have your Values with you when creating your Vision.
- You can have things in your Vision that don't fit into any of your Values, because there's a section called 'Other' for those things.
- Unlike your Purpose and Mission, your Vision is always added to over time. Your Vision will become many pages long.
- Be conscious of when you 'space out' and visualise your future. That's when you're literally downloading bits of your Vision.
- Don't add things into your Vision that aren't actually yours.

Don't let other people project their Values on to you, on what you 'should' have in your Vision. Be you.

Steps for Creating Your Vision:

1. Schedule in at least 30 minutes to do this process properly.
2. Write down your Values in order in the spaces provided.
3. Expand on what your Values will look like in 5-10 years (once you've achieved the Mission). Be as detailed as possible. Make it so real that you feel it.
4. Use the 'Other' section to add anything that's in your Vision that doesn't fit into your current Values.
5. Read over your Vision and magnify the emotions you feel as you feel them.
6. Use your Vision to create a Vision board. (I will provide a template.)

I have provided an example of my Vision as inspiration on page 261. I have only provided my Vision for three of my Values to save space. Make sure you do all of yours.

Put your answers in the Vision section on page 267

Step 1: Add your Values in the spaces provided. If you have fewer or more than what's provided, that's okay. Just write the extras elsewhere.

Step 2: Expand on what your Values will look like in 5 -10 years. Be as detailed as possible. Also use the 'Other' section for things that don't fit into your Values.

Congratulations! You've now created your Life's Vision! Now, if you'd like to translate this written Vision into a Vision board, I highly recommend it. Here is a link to a Vision board template you can use:

www.lewishuckstep.com/book (and click on the 'Vision Board' tab)

Of course, if you have other software you'd prefer to use, please do that. Use Google or even AI to get images that represent each part of your Vision. Download those images, then drag and drop them into the template I've provided. Super simple. Then I recommend setting it as a background for your computer or phone, or just have it somewhere where you will see it daily. You could also print out a copy.

As always, let me now show you a real-life example of how knowing your life's Mission and Vision can change your life forever.

Savana is a soon-to-be personal trainer on the Gold Coast. She is a very motivated and driven woman, but she really lacked the clarity of what she truly wanted for her life. When I met Sav, she had a media job in which she wasn't happy. She had studied at university to work in the media industry, so she thought she 'had to' get a job doing this.

When we worked together, we got clear on her Values, her Purpose and her life's Mission and Vision. Surprise, surprise – her Mission and Vision had no alignment with what she was doing at her job but, with the new-found clarity, Sav was able firstly to get a job in the industry she loved (fitness) and then she was able to build her own business within this industry.

In her words, "I didn't realise until I worked on and wrote out my Mission, Values and Purpose, that I was in the wrong career. I have now made the transition into my dream career and I'm living my most Inspired Life. I've also created a business that is authentically me."

How cool is that? All from getting clear on who she authentically was (Values and Purpose) and getting clear on what she truly wanted (Mission and Vision). If you'd like to watch the full video yourself, just use this link: https://youtu.be/hn7Q0JbHZPU or scan this QR code:

Figure 8

Summary of Mission:

1. It's a big five- to ten-year goal.

2. It has something measurable which can be broken down into actionable steps. (We're about to do that in the coming chapters.)

3. It gives you enough time to get through the 'crisis of meaning' stage.

Summary of Vision:

1. It's a detailed description of what your life looks like once you've hit your Mission.

2. You expand on your Values to create your Vision.

3. Be aware of when you zone out and see your future because you're downloading parts of your Vision.

Quick Recap:

We've covered a lot of ground already. You now know what truly fulfils you and who you authentically are (your Values); you know your gift to give to the world and in what direction to head (your Purpose); and you have a clear measurable destination to pursue (Mission and Vision). You need a couple more pieces to unlock your inspired life.

Those remaining pieces are:

1. Clarity of how much money you need to earn to live your Dream Life. (We're doing that in the next chapter.)
2. Selecting the right vehicle that aligns with your Purpose and allows you to earn the money needed.
3. Your bulletproof Master Plan on exactly what needs to get done to fulfil your Vision.
4. Doing the Inner Work to stop any self-sabotaging that will stop you from following the plan.

You're doing so well. Give yourself a little pat on the back and then let's continue.

The next question is: *How much money do I need and how do I make money living out my Purpose and Mission?* What a great question. Let's find that answer together.

CHAPTER 5
Dream Life and Income Needed

*"Money isn't the most important thing in life,
but it's reasonably close to oxygen..."*

- Zig Ziglar

Now I don't 100% agree with this quote; however, I've experienced what life is like with no money. Seeing my parents constantly fight over money, worrying that I won't have enough money to afford petrol, having anxiety about checking my bank account and even going without food because I was completely broke. It causes so much stress and pressure in all areas of life.

Once I confronted my fear around money, learnt about it and actually gained clarity on how to earn the amount I needed to live my Dream Life – doing what I loved – the anxiety went away because I knew I had the ability to achieve it. Remember that money just magnifies who you are. If you're a mean person, you'll have more to be mean with. If you're a giving person, you'll have more to give with.

Picture this:

The exact amount of money you need to live your Dream Life pours into your bank account every single week. You spend your days with the people that you love, doing what you love. You work because you want to, not because you have to. This isn't a pipe dream, it's a life that you're worthy of living. You just need to know how much money you need to earn to live it.

Let's figure out how to do that.

How to Create Your Dream Life and the Income Needed

We've done the fluffy, emotional, intrinsic things (excluding the Inner Work from Chapter 9 onwards), so it's time to get more tactical and practical. Given the world we live in, you need to have absolute clarity of how much it will realistically cost you to live your Dream Life. Unfortunately, you can't pay your rent with love, trust and pixie dust and, unless we evolve into a society that uses a different form of value exchange for goods and services, money will remain a pivotal piece of creating your Dream Life.

So, how do we work out how much your Dream Life will cost? First, we need to be clear on what this looks like on a daily/weekly/monthly basis. We also need to clarify the difference between your 'Vision' and your 'Dream Life'.

Vision is the bigger picture of what your life looks like.

Dream Life is describing the details of what your day-to-day life looks like, so you can figure out how much it will cost you to create it.

Let's create your Dream Life.

For some inspiration for designing your Dream Life, consider the following areas of life and potential things to add into your own.

Probing topics/questions:

- What type of home do you want to live in?

- What car do you want to drive?

- How much travel do you want to have?

- Necessities (food, clothing, bills, etc).

- Education/self-development.

- Team members, personal or professional (cleaner, personal chef, nanny, assistant, personal trainer, etc).

- Luxuries (clothes, cars, technology, supplements, etc.).

Rules for Designing Your Dream Life:

- Use your Vision as inspiration for this exercise.

- Describe what your day-to-day and week-to-week life will actually look like.

- Create this from inspiration and not fear. Don't use money as a constraint. Think, 'If money wasn't a factor, what life would I live?'

- Use the first person – 'I live in my dream home on the beach, with my dream partner with our three beautiful children. I drive my dream car, a Lamborghini. I train every morning with my personal trainer. I get weekly massages from my personal masseuse. I travel first class with my family for two months every year.'

- Don't put things into your Dream Life that are not yours. The more times I do this exercise, the simpler my Dream Life becomes.

- This exercise has the least amount of guidance. This really is for you to sit with your own thoughts and dreams about what you truly desire. Use the probing topics and questions to help.

Use the following space (or somewhere else if you prefer) to design your Dream Life from a daily, weekly, monthly, quarterly and yearly perspective.

My Dream Life:

_____

_____

_____

_____

_____

_____

_____

_____

_____

_____

_____

_____

Well done! For the next step, let's work out how much it will cost to live that Dream Life. To do this, just do some good old-fashioned Googling with a calculator or even use AI to help. I suggest getting clear on what the weekly figure is for each of the things you have in your Dream Life. (Some people prefer monthly or even yearly, but weekly works best for my mind.) I also suggest going to websites to see how much the type of house or car, or whatever it is that you want, actually costs to maintain weekly (or whatever timescale you're using). I've provided a table for you (TABLE 3), and I've also created an online tool and training if you prefer to use that instead. Go to this link:

www.lewishuckstep.com/book or just scan the QR code below:

TABLE 3	Cost per week (or whatever time measurement you're using)	Description
House/s		
Car/s		
Travel		
Necessities		
Education		
Team		
Luxuries		
Other		

Now add up those numbers and write the total here:

The cost of my Dream Life is: $ _____ per (week/month/year).

Crushed it! Now, you might be someone who thinks, *How do I earn that much money? I don't earn anything close to that now.* That's okay. That's why we're on this journey together. We're going to be answering that question in the very next chapter.

To give you another perspective, let me tell you about Ryan, an 11-year-old boy who loves toys. Ryan Kaji became the youngest person to make the Forbes top earners list, raking in $11 million at the age of six ... no, that's not a typo. He continued to grow and expand his successes, and at the ripe old age of 11 he took in a respectable $27 million in 2021.[4]

If you are wondering how this boy made more money than 99 percent of other people on the planet at the age of 11 ... he has a YouTube channel reviewing toys!! Yes, he – along with other activities – reviews toys. What you're about to learn is the power of <u>leverage</u> – the ingredient you need to earn the money you require for your Dream Life.

> *"Give me a lever long enough and a fulcrum on which to place it, and I shall move the world."*
>
> **– Archimedes**

Summary of Dream Life and Income Needed:

1. Your Dream Life is what your day-to-day life is like in your Vision.

2. Getting clear on the actual income needed for your Dream Life makes it possible to achieve it.

3. It is possible to earn the amount of money needed to live your Dream Life. (There's an 11-year-old who's doing it!)

Let's figure out how to make that money needed to live your Dream Life.

---

[4] Forbes, "Ryan Kaji," Forbes, accessed September 2, 2024, https://www.forbes.com/profile/ryan-kaji/?sh=25a489896f3c.

CHAPTER 6

CashFlow Quadrant and Selecting the Right Vehicle

"It doesn't matter how hard you row.
It matters which boat you get in."

— Warren Buffett

I dropped out of university after reading this book...

I was in my final year of school, senior year (I actually repeated my senior year to keep up with the study.) I'd attended all the career days where they expose students to all the career paths available after completing school, but nothing really stood out to me. I had no clue what I wanted to do, and I couldn't answer the question I was asked most often in my final year: "What are you going to do when you finish school?" It really frustrated me.

In that critical time between the ages of 16 and 18 – when we are burdened with those lifelong decisions that will significantly dictate our future – most of us will receive very little support to help determine what we truly want to do.

Regardless of how I felt, decisions had to be made. I did what I thought made the most sense. I liked training (sports background) and I had some life-changing teachers who had acted in many ways as father figures and who changed my life. So, I decided I'd become a high school teacher and a personal trainer. I decided I could teach PE (physical exercise/sports teacher) and be a personal trainer in the holidays to make more money. Epic. My life plan was locked and loaded.

Boy, was I wrong!

With about four months left until I had finished school forever, I decided to start on the personal training pathway by getting a job as a trainer at a gym. I applied at eight gyms and even got a trial at one, but all of them rejected me, explaining that I did not have enough experience. I was wondering, *How do you get any experience if no one will hire you?*

I gave up on that dream for about a month but then a friend, who was a year younger than me, did get a job at a gym. I honestly thought I was better, so I decided to put myself back out there.

For whatever reason I jumped on an app called Gumtree. In Australia, especially in 2015, it was mainly used to sell used belongings, like couches and cars. But, as fortune had it, there was a job vacancy advertised by a gym called PLC. I called the person on the ad and said, "I'm not looking to get paid; I'm just looking for work experience. Can I come and work for free?" Scott, the owner, said, "Absolutely. Come down and meet me at the gym so we can chat." That phone call changed my life forever.

I started working for free to gain experience. I still had the plan to become a teacher and be a personal trainer before and after school hours and during the holidays. While doing my work experience at the gym, I finished my final year of school, and I was then accepted into university to become a high school teacher.

Things were going to plan. Scott, who was my first mentor, was constantly listening to self-development podcasts, reading books and attending these weird motivational seminars. Because I looked up to him, I was very curious about what these were and why he did them. He started to send me some YouTube clips to watch. The videos featured an American named Tony Robbins. I remember that the first video I watched was all about building rapport and how to connect with others. *Wow, why aren't we taught this in school?* I asked myself after watching it. I started consuming these videos as often as I could. It was so stimulating and empowering to learn so many mindset and emotional tools that I could use in my day-to-day life.

Scott gave me a book called *Rich Dad Poor Dad* [5], about a young Robert Kiyosaki growing up with two fathers. His biological father – a highly educated man, who ultimately ended up broke – and his friend's father, who dropped out of high school but ended up being one of the wealthiest people in Hawaii.

This book shifted the way I viewed the world. The traditional path of going to school, maybe going to university, getting a high-paying job, working there for 40+ years, getting a mortgage, building up a superannuation (401K for my American friends, or just a retirement fund), retiring and living off a retirement fund until dying ... made no sense after reading this book.

At that time, my key three lessons from his book (and from his second book *Rich Dad Poor Dad's Cashflow Quadrant*) were:

1. The rich don't work for money; they have money work for them.
2. The wealthy have access to tax benefits that the middle class do not.
3. The importance of leverage. If you don't learn how to leverage your time for more money, you will never be free.

Robert Kiyosaki often refers to *the rat race*, and by rat race he means the trap that most of the world falls into – that if you want to make more money, you need to work longer and harder. But there are only so many hours in the day you can work. And if you ever decide to stop work, or you are forced to stop, you stop earning income. Hence, you're stuck in a never-ending rat race to try to get ahead.

My 18-year-old mind was blown away. I'd spent all those years being conditioned to believe that the rat race was normal and even

---

[5] Rich Dad, "Rich Dad Education," accessed September 2, 2024, https://www.richdad.com/.

expected. I had a decision to make. I could either continue down the teacher plus personal trainer route – which offered more certainty, but ultimately would lead to the rat race – or I could commit to the journey with my mentor to build a business that had an incredibly high chance of failure (90% of businesses fail after 10 years). I would have to face my fears and insecurities, but doing so could give me the leverage I needed to create my Dream Life.

Thankfully, I took the second option. I told the university I was dropping out, and I went all in on building my business. This decision led me down an eight-year path of owning three gyms by the age of 22, hitting breaking points of crying my eyes out – the story I shared in Chapter One – but eventually building a business that paid me $2000–$3000 a week for one hour of work. I now have a full-time income through living my Purpose. The lessons with which Robert Kiyosaki blessed me are what I want to pass on to you. They are needed if you want to create a life on your terms.

CashFlow Quadrant

The following diagram is what Robert Kiyosaki calls the CashFlow Quadrant:

Figure 9[6]

Now, this simple diagram has so much value – I could talk about it for days. But instead of me doing that, read the book, *Rich Dad Poor Dad's Cashflow Quadrant*, if you want to take a deep dive into the power of this simple framework. In the meantime, I will explain the three biggest takeaways that apply to everything we've already covered so far together.

First, let me explain what each letter represents and means:

---

[6] Jeff Anzalone, "Robert Kiyosaki Cashflow Quadrant: Everything You Need to Know," *Debt Free Dr.*, accessed Septemver 2, 2024, https://www.debtfreedr.com/robert-kiyosaki-cashflow-quadrant/.

E = Employee. You have a job where you work and get paid a salary. **Using time to make money**.

S = Self-employed. You own a job, meaning you have a business, but the business depends on you. If you stopped working and your business would go backwards then you don't own a business, you own a job. **S** also represents **Speciality**, meaning you have a high-paying job like a doctor, lawyer or any other high-income job. **S** also represents **Stars,** meaning celebrities or athletes. **Using time to make money**.

B = Business Owner. You own a business (asset) that runs without you (or with a very minimal amount of work from you), that pays you income every week and that has the potential for its value to increase. **Using systems and other people to make money**.

I = Investor. You own assets (stocks, real estate, businesses) that pay you money or go up in value, without you doing anything. **Using money to make more money**.

Now, here are the three biggest takeaways I mentioned, and what you need to know in order to create your Dream Life.

1. **Trading time for money.** The left-hand side of the CashFlow Quadrant, the **E**'s (Employee) and the **S**'s (Self-employed, speciality, stars), are about trading time for money. If you stop working, you stop earning income. Therefore, you will never get out of the rat race. The right side of the quadrant, the **B**'s (Business owners) and **I**'s (Investors) use systems, other people and money to make money. So, the **B**'s and **I**'s are able to make money <u>without</u> using their time.

   In the short term, obviously you need to invest your time to build a business or have enough money to be able to invest; however, the path to time and financial freedom is on the right-hand side of the quadrant.

   Now, don't misunderstand me, there is nothing wrong with working at a job or being self-employed doing something that you're super passionate about where you trade time for money. But, if it won't allow you to earn the income needed to live your Dream Life, then you'll never be able to get to the Dream Life that you created in the previous chapter.

Before we use the word leverage, let's define it. As Archimedes said, "*Give me a lever long enough and a fulcrum on which to place it, and I shall move the world.*" Leverage can be defined as **the difference between what you put in versus what you get out.** You can put one in and get one out or you can put one in and get 10 out. The difference is the leverage of the activity (vehicle) that you're doing. We will revisit leverage when we get to the Master Planning section.

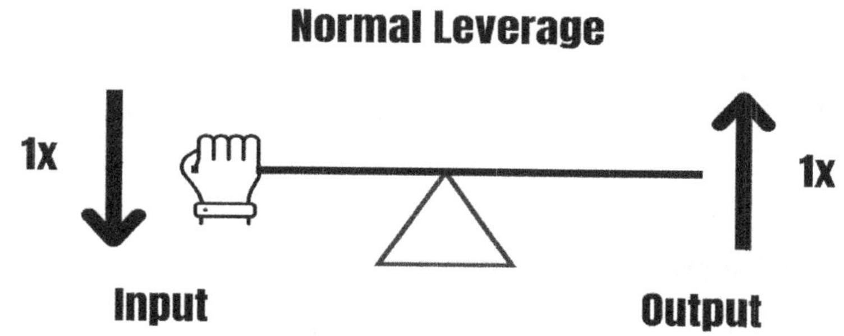

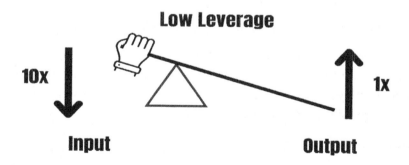

Normal Leverage

1x — Input

1x — Output

Figure 10.1

Low Leverage

10x — Input

1x — Output

Figure 10.2

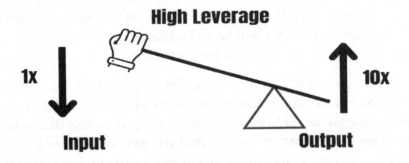

High Leverage

1x

Input

10x

Output

Figure 10.3

2. **Leverage/scaling income.** The left-hand side of the quadrant is very limited in leverage and scalability in relation to how much money you can earn. You might work at a job for years, in the hopes of getting a pay rise of a couple dollars or more per hour. That's nice, but you're still very limited. However, the right-hand side of the quadrant has uncapped earning potential. Let's use an example:

Employee example:

You are an employee, and you get paid $30 per hour.

If you worked a 38-hour week you will make $1,140.

If you worked a 50-hour week you will make $1,900.

If you worked an 80-hour week you will make $2,400.

Yes, you can also increase how much you earn depending on your role, compensation plan and company structure, but your income is still dependent on your time, and it's very hard to increase how much you earn because of the lack of leverage.

Business owner example:

You own a business that sells online courses, and you make $30 profit per sale.

88

If you sell 38 units in a week you will make $1,140.

If you sell 50 units in a week you will make $1,900.

If you sell 80 units in a week you will make $2,400.

If you sell 200 units in a week you will make $6,000.

If you sell 5000 units in a week you will make $150,000.

If you sell 10,000 units in a week you will make $300,000.

You can see how the income you can make is so much more scalable versus trading your time for money. Also, in this business example, you can have systems and be paying people to do all of the work, leaving you free to do whatever inspires you , some of which might involve working in the business because that's what you love. That's awesome. I love working within my coaching business, so I do the things I love, and I delegate the rest.

3. **Tax Benefits**. I will start this point by stating that I am not an accountant, and this is not financial advice. Please speak to an accountant about your specific situation when it comes to tax. However, one of the biggest advantages of being on the right side of the quadrant, is having access to so many legal tax loopholes and benefits. For example, you can have company structures where you can offset a lot of the tax that you pay and also claim a lot of your living expenses against tax. (Again, this is getting very tactical, and these conversations need to be with your accountants and other professionals.)

So, what does this all mean for you?

If the way that you currently earn income will not allow you to earn the amount needed to live your Dream Life, then you need to change your strategy, which will probably involve you moving into a different section of the CashFlow Quadrant. This means 'selecting the right vehicle' that aligns with your Dream Life.

Selecting the Right Vehicle

The term 'vehicle' in this context refers to the way you generate income or cash flow. In the case of the employee trading time for money, the job is their vehicle. For a business owner, the business is their vehicle. As you can already see, different vehicles have significantly different benefits and drawbacks. So, to be able to decide which vehicle is best for you, you need to know which vehicle has the capacity to get you to your destination (your Dream Life/Vision).

Before picking the specific vehicle for your journey, there are three empowered pathways for you to consider and one disempowered pathway, which I hope you don't do. They all have their pros and cons.

The Three Empowered Pathways

1. **Find a career that is aligned with your Purpose:** Know your Values and Purpose, then get work in a role and with a company that is really aligned with them.

Pros:

- **Less Risk of Failure:** You don't have to go out and start a business and put yourself in a position where you can fail in front of others and potentially lose money.

- **Guaranteed Income:** Depending on the role and the compensation plan, you will have more of a guaranteed income.

- **Skill Development:** Jobs often provide opportunities for skill development and career advancement, and you'll be getting paid to learn.

- **Work-Life Balance:** Depending on the job and employer, there may be better-defined work hours, allowing for a more consistent work-life balance.

- **Benefits:** Many employers offer benefits such as health insurance, retirement plans and paid time off.

Cons:

- **Limited Income Potential:** Income is usually capped by salary or hourly wage, limiting potential earnings.

- **Limited Control:** Employees have less control over their work tasks, schedule and the company's overall direction.

- **Job Insecurity:** There's always a risk of layoffs, downsizing, or being replaced, especially in volatile industries.

- **Less Flexibility:** Jobs may offer less flexibility in terms of work hours, location and holiday time.

- **Limited Creativity:** Depending on the job, there may be limited opportunities for creativity and innovation.

The next two options have similar pros and cons, as they are the same fundamental vehicle (business). The difference is you can either monetise your Purpose or you just build any business to give you the freedom to live your Purpose without the need to monetise it.

2. **Build a business that is an expression of your Purpose:** Build a Purpose-led business. Build a business that allows you to express your Purpose by giving it back to others. '*When what you do is the fullest expression of who you are, you will do your life's best work*.' You build this business around the things you want to do, and you delegate the rest.

3. **Build any business that gives you enough cash flow, so you don't need to work anymore: Invest your time building up any business to give you the income needed to live your Dream Life.** You'll have time and financial freedom. (If you end up doing this option, you'll often find yourself '*living your Purpose*' because you have the freedom to do so and you might end up monetising it as well. This is the path I unconsciously took with the gyms.)

Pros:

- **Unlimited Income Potential**: Entrepreneurs have the opportunity to earn unlimited income based on the success of their business.

- **Autonomy**: Business owners have full control over their work, including decision-making, creative direction and business strategy.

- **Flexibility**: Running a business offers flexibility in terms of work hours, location and overall schedule.

- **Personal Fulfilment**: Starting and growing a successful business can be personally fulfilling and rewarding.

- **Growth/Impact Opportunities**: Entrepreneurs have the potential to scale their business and impact, expand into new markets, and grow their brand and network.

- **Freedom Long Term:** Once your business matures and you delegate the roles needed, you can have time and financial freedom, where you only work because you want to and not because you have to.

Cons:

- **Financial Risk**: Starting a business involves financial risk, including losing money and going into debt.

- **Uncertainty**: The success of a business is not guaranteed, and there's always uncertainty surrounding market conditions, consumer demand and competition.

- **Long Hours**: Business owners often work long hours, especially in the early stages of building their company.

- **Responsibility**: Entrepreneurs bear the ultimate responsibility for the success or failure of their business, which can be stressful and demanding.

The One Disempowered Pathway:

There are many variants of this, but you'll understand the core of it.

1. **Work at a career that you don't love, and never change.** We all start somewhere. My first job was at McDonalds, which is great if you love it, but I wasn't passionate about it at all. It was just a job to pay bills. If you are doing a job that you don't love and you're not actively looking to change that, you are going to be miserable for a massive part of your life. We spend on average one-third of our lives working.[7] Please don't pick this option.

There is technically a fourth pathway to be an Investor (the **I** from the CashFlow Quadrant), but it's less common to start here because you need money to make money. It's also risky because you can lose money if you don't know what you're doing; however, a lot of skills from the **B** section (Business Owner) translate over to the **I** section. Look at the difference in these two scenarios:

Scenario 1:

You work at a job, and you invest $400 a month (which is also amazing to get started with) into the S&P 500 (stock market) for 50 years with a 7.5% average return.[8] You will end up with $2,409,597. Of that, $2,169,197 is interest. In other words, your money will have made you more than $2 million.

---

[7] Gettysburg College, "The Average Person Will Spend 90,000 Hours at Work Over a Lifetime," Gettysburg College News, accessed September 2, 2024, https://www.gettysburg.edu/news/stories?id=79db7b34-630c-4f49-ad32-4ab9ea48e72b#:~:text=The%20average%20person%20will%20spend%2090%2C000%20hours%20at%20work%20over%20a%20lifetime.

[8] Chris Davis, "What Is the Average Stock Market Return?," *NerdWallet*, last modified June 26, 2023, https://www.nerdwallet.com/article/investing/average-stock-market-return.

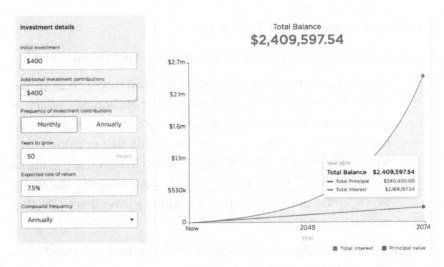

Figure 11

Scenario 2:

You own a business, and you invest $4,000 a month into the S&P 500 for 50 years with a 7.5% average return. You will end up with $24,095,975. Of that, $21,691,975 is interest. In other words, your money made you more than $21 million.

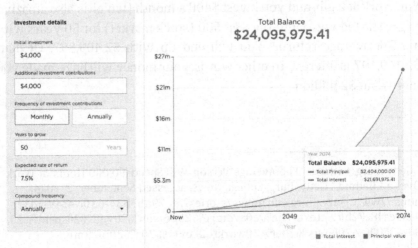

Figure 12

For the same effort and time doing the investing, you end up with an extra $19 million. Why? Because you have more money to invest. So, unless you have specific investment strategies, have access to a lot of money, or you already have a thriving business, I'd suggest focusing on the other three pathways first. Also, if you decide to do pathway one and build a career aligned with your Values and Purpose, I would highly recommend investing your money, but remember, this is not financial advice.

Decision Time

When making your decisions in this chapter, use this framework to help you decide.

1. What do you love? (Use your Values and Purpose to help with this.)
2. What are your skills and talents?
3. What can you make an income at by solving problems? (There are probably more ways that you might think to do this. Remember the 11-year-old Ryan.)
4. What is the triple intersection of these (see Fig. 13.)?

Figure 13

So, with all this information, there are a few big decisions you need to make, and each pathway has different follow-up decisions. I will lay out the three empowered pathways with their follow-up decisions. Decide which one is for you and complete the relevant questions. I'd recommend reading this entire chapter through before deciding and then writing your answers.

Pathway 1: Find a career aligned with your Purpose.

1. **What do I truly love doing? Use your Values and Purpose to help with this.**

   _____

   _____

   _____

   _____

2. **What am I good at and what problems can I solve?**

   _____

   _____

   _____

   _____

3. **What job/career allows me to fulfil the answers from questions one and two?**

   _____

   _____

   _____

   _____

Here are some bonus tips to consider when looking for the right career pathway for you:

- Does this role/company have a healthy culture?

- Does this role/company have growth pathways available, personally and professionally?

Pathway 2: Build a business that is an expression of your Purpose.

1. **What do I truly love doing? Use your Values and Purpose to help with this.**

   _____

   _____

   _____

   _____

2. **What am I good at and what problems can I solve?**

   _____

   _____

   _____

   _____

3. **What business model allows me to fulfil the answers from questions one and two? There are so many different business models to consider. (See below and over the page for options to consider)**

   _____

   _____

   _____

   _____

Pathway 3: Build any business that gives you enough cash flow, so you don't need to work anymore.

1. **What am I good at and what problems can I solve?**

   _____

   _____

   _____

   _____

2. **What world industries are currently growing?**

   _____

   _____

   _____

   _____

3. **What business model matches my strengths the most and is within a growing industry? (See below and over the page for options to consider)**

   _____

   _____

   _____

   _____

List of Business Models to Consider:

- **Content Creator (YouTube, Podcasting, Blogging):** Creating and sharing valuable content online to build an audience and generate revenue through ads, sponsorships and affiliate marketing.

- **Coaching/Mentoring:** Offering personalised guidance and expertise in various fields such as business, fitness, personal development, etc.

- **Online Service Business (Graphic Design, Web Development, Virtual Assistance, AI services):** Providing services remotely to clients worldwide through platforms like Upwork, Freelancer or independently.

- **Freelancing (Writing, Graphic Design, Programming):** Offering specialised skills on a project basis through freelancing platforms or direct client outreach.

- **Streaming (Twitch, Facebook Gaming):** Broadcasting live content, such as gaming, art creation or commentary, and earn revenue through subscriptions, donations and sponsorships.

- **Photography/Videography:** Capturing and selling images or videos for commercial use, events, stock photography or content creation.

- **Content Editing/Writing:** Providing editing and writing services for individuals, businesses or publications.

- **Drop shipping/E-commerce:** Selling products online without holding inventory, by partnering with suppliers who handle shipping and fulfilment.

- **Trading/Investing (Stocks, Cryptocurrency, Forex):** Speculating on financial markets to generate returns through buying, selling or holding assets.

- **Real Estate Investing (Rental Properties, Flipping):** Buying, renting or renovating properties for profit through appreciation, rental income or resale.

- **E-Learning (Online Courses, Workshops):** Creating and selling educational content and resources on specific topics or skills.

- **Pet Services (Sitting, Grooming, Training):** Offering pet-care services such as pet-sitting, grooming, training or even creating pet-related products.

- **Network Marketing/Direct Sales:** Selling products or services directly to consumers and building a team to earn commissions on sales and recruitment.

- **Affiliate Marketing:** Promoting products or services for other companies and earning a commission on sales generated through affiliate links.

- **Ride-Sharing/Delivery (Uber, Lyft, DoorDash©):** Providing transport or delivery services through app-based platforms.

- **Tutoring/Teaching (Language, Academic Subjects):** Providing personalised instruction and guidance to students in various subjects or skills.

- **Flipping (Garage Sales, Thrift Stores):** Buying low-cost items and reselling them at a higher price for profit, either online or through physical stores.

- **Franchise Ownership:** Buying the rights to operate a proven business model under an established brand name.

- **Traditional Business (Brick-and-Mortar):** Establishing and running a physical storefront or service-based business in a specific location.

- **Short-term Rental (Airbnb, Vacation Rentals):** Renting out properties or rooms to travellers for short-term stays, often through online platforms.

- **Digital Marketing Agency:** Providing digital marketing services such as social media management, search engine optimisation (SEO) and content marketing for businesses.

Every one of these has its pros and cons. There is no easy business model where you do seven magical steps, tickle the genie's belly, then money just flows into your bank account while you kick back and drink margaritas on the beach. Remember 90% of businesses fail in the first 10 years.[9] However, by actually taking the time to consider what you love and what you're good at and weighing up the pros and cons of each option, you're stacking the odds in your favour.

Depending on where you are on your journey and what your current skill set is, the business models I'd recommend considering would have:

- Low barrier to entry – it doesn't cost you much to start.

- Low overheads – very low cost to run.

- The ability to scale through the internet – you can help more people, and you're not restricted to where you live.

Of the options suggested, these are the ones I would explore if I was starting afresh:

- An online service-based business – coaching, mentoring, marketing agency, AI agency, etc.

- Network marketing.

As I mentioned near the beginning of this book, the Skills and Strategies pillar of *The Inspired Life Method* is too broad to cram into one book, which is why we are covering the core foundational aspects of the method. However, if you're asking, *"How do I start and build my business to give me time and financial freedom?"* such specific questions won't be answered here, but I do address those questions in my Conscious Community (details of which I'll share towards the end of this book).

---

[9] Josh Howarth, "Startup Failure Rate: How Many Startups Fail and Why?," *Exploding Topics,* last modified June 20, 2023, https://explodingtopics.com/blog/startup-failure-stats.

Real-Life Example

Here's a story of the investor Warren Buffett and his journey from being an employee, to a business owner, then to being an investor.[10] We can see how the leverage of his wealth increased each time he moved into a different vehicle and section of the CashFlow Quadrant.

At the age of 15 he was earning more than $175 a month delivering newspapers. He was operating as an Employee, which is where most people start their journey. In 1954 (when he was 24), he landed a job at Benjamin Graham's partnership, earning a modest salary of $12,000 a year (about $131,000 in 2024). He was operating out of the S section (Specialty) of the CashFlow Quadrant.

In 1962 (aged 31) through his partnerships (business owner), Buffett became a millionaire. This happened because he was using a vehicle with more leverage. This also gave him the resources and even more leverage. Allowing him to become an investor, which is what he is best known for today.

In his mid-40s, Buffett had faced financial challenges, with his net worth dropping to $19 million. However, his resilience and investment skills allowed him to recover, increasing his net worth to $67 million by age 47. In 1986, at age 56, Buffett's net worth had grown to the point where he became a billionaire.[11] By January 2024 (now 93 years old), Warren's net worth was $122 billion.[12] That's the power of using the right vehicle with leverage.

---

[10] Warren Buffet," Wikipedia, last modified September 1, 2024, Warren Buffet," *Wikipedia,* last modified September 1, 2024, https://en.wikipedia.org/wiki/Warren_Buffett.

[11] Theron Mohamed, "Warren Buffett Accumulated 99% of His Wealth After His 50th Birthday - and His Net Worth Has Grown by $100 Billion in the Past Three Years," *Yahoo Finance,* last modified August 22, 2023, https://finance.yahoo.com/news/warren-buffett-accumulated-99-net-193522940.html.

[12] "Warren Buffett," *Wikipedia.*

Would Buffett ever have become a billionaire if he had stayed at his newspaper delivery job? Absolutely not. His story is a prime example of the power of leverage and also the power of compounding growth.

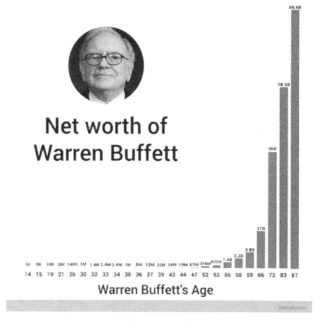

Net worth of Warren Buffett

Warren Buffett's Age

Figure 14[13]

Summary of Selecting the Right Vehicle:

1. Be aware of which vehicle you need to be able to earn the income necessary for your Dream Life.

2. There are three empowered pathways to choose from. Pick wisely.

3. Leverage is your best friend.

[13] Diego Ruzzarin, "Warren Buffett Has Made 99.7% of His Money After the Age of 52," *Medium,* The 10X Entrepreneur (blog), January 15, 2023, https://medium.com/the-10x-entrepreneur/warren-buffett-has-made-99-7-of-his-money-after-the-age-of-52-71e2ce04c347.

Well done for all your work so far. What's next on our journey to live an inspired life? Putting this all into action and making it all real. Creating your life's Master Plan. This is where "the rubber meets the road", and you actually start acting to make all this come to life.

Let's do it.

CHAPTER 7

Master Planning

If you're taking action but you're not making more money. You're working on the wrong shit.

Alex, a young, motivated man in his mid-20s, had more energy than anyone you've met. He was driven, focused, determined and willing to do whatever it took to be successful. He had worked 12 to 14 hours every day of the week, harder than anyone else he had met. He came from a broken family that struggled with money, and his parents were abusive to each other and the children. His dad left when Alex was only 10 years old – Core wound.

Alex had a lot of fuel to support his mother who sacrificed so much for him. Every morning, he would jump out of bed to pursue his goals of being a successful entrepreneur, to be able to support his mother and future family, but Alex was all over the place. One day he would be sprinting in a certain direction, then he would get some advice from someone through a conversation or a book, and he would immediately start sprinting in another direction. This had been going on for almost seven years. What really frustrated Alex was that he wasn't trying different businesses, so he felt he wasn't suffering from 'shiny object syndrome'. A mentor had taught him the importance of sticking to an opportunity for a long enough time to allow the compounding effects to happen.

Because of his potent fuel (Purpose) to provide for his family, Alex would not give up. He wouldn't let the lack of results stop him from taking action. One day he saw an ad on his social media about a free seminar called 'Life Master Planning – Get the absolute clarity you need *to build a successful life'*. Alex was not new to seminars – he had been attending them since he was 17 – so he grabbed a ticket.

At the seminar Alex felt really inspired but also disappointed. He met a lot of people who were making a lot more money and were more successful than he was. They were all working fewer hours with less effort. Alex started beating himself up. *'Maybe there's something wrong with me. Maybe I'm just not meant to be successful,'* he started telling himself. After meeting another five people who were more successful but didn't work as hard as he did, he thought: *If these guys can do it, I can do it. I just need to figure out what I'm missing.*

The seminar started to get into the core of the content, and the speaker did a little activity with the crowd:

"Raise your hand if you've been working really hard at the same thing for at least more than six months," he told them. Most of the crowd, including Alex, put their hands up.

"Now keep your hand up if you're <u>not</u> making more money now than six months ago." Surprisingly, most of the crowd, including Alex, kept their hands up.

"If your hand is in the air, you are working on the wrong shit, you're not taking the right action you need to be taking," the speaker said in a powerful, penetrating voice. "Now, keep your hand in the air if you <u>don't</u> have a REAL detailed growth plan for your business/life, and if you were to show me your plan, I would approve that it's a REAL plan." Again, most of the hands remained in the air. Alex started to realise.

"If you fail to plan, you're planning to fail," said the speaker, with a dramatic pause to let the message sink in, before going on. "Ten to 12 minutes invested in planning your day will save at least two hours of wasted time and effort throughout the day.[14] If you're not actively

---

[14] Cornerstone Dynamics, "Time Management Stats That May Surprise You," last modified July 2023, https://www.cornerstonedynamics.com/time-management-stats-that-may-surprise-you

planning your business life or personal life and are constantly course correcting the plan, you are driving a car with no map. How do you think you're actually going to make progress to where you want to go?"

Alex was speechless – the countless times he had been told, "If you fail to plan, you plan to fail", yet he didn't actually do it. He felt like an idiot, but at the same time felt so empowered because he knew clearly that he already had the will to do what needed to be done.

At the seminar, Alex went through the 'Life Master Planning Process' and came out with a whole new perspective. He couldn't believe that he'd spent his life up to that point just reacting to what he thought was the best thing to do, which was very dependent on how he felt at that moment. Alex, now equipped with his new bulletproof plan – five years, three years, two years, 12 months, quarterly, weekly and daily outcomes – went on to dominate his business and reach his personal life goals. He grew his business to a point where he retired and had the freedom to spend time with his family when he chose. That's the power of planning.

The Life Master Planning Process

"Complexity is the enemy of execution."
– Anthony Robbins

If you want to create your Dream Life, you need to know what your Dream Life is and how much it costs to live it (done). You need to have the fuel (Purpose) to drive you to take the action needed (done). You need to have a clearly defined measurable goal (Mission) so you can reverse engineer it (done). You then need the right vehicle to allow you to fulfil the Mission (done). You finally need to break down that goal into a step-by-step actionable plan (Master Plan). Let's do that now.

The reason that planning is so essential is that it allows you to be strategic with your decisions and actions. Let's define strategy:

Strategy *"is the allocation of limited resources against unlimited options."*

– Alex Hormozi [15]

Everyone has a limited amount of resources, some have more than others but there is a limit for everyone. If you're just starting out, you probably have very limited resources compared to someone like Jeff Bezos who, as of February 2024, had a net worth of $197 billion dollars. [16] So, with the unlimited options but limited resources, you must be sure about what decisions and actions you intend to take.

I used to think that successful people were just crazy productive workers who could get 10 times more work done in a day than I could. To me, these people could type insanely fast, handle five projects at once, never need sleep and were special in some way that I was not. In reality, they were just really good at knowing the highest leverage activity to do. They said *no* to all the other shiny objects, they delegated what they could with whatever resources they had, and they relentlessly focused on doing the highest leverage activity for them at that stage on their journey.

Let's revisit leverage:

The difference between what you put in and what you get out.

---

[15] Alex Hormozi, "Why Your Business Should Be Like an Airport," *TikTok* video, 0.58, posted January 2, 2023, https://www.tiktok.com/@ahormozi/video/7182694253749914926.
[16] "Jeff Bezos," *Wikipedia*, last modified September 1, 2024, ,https://en.wikipedia.org/wiki/Jeff_Bezos.

Normal Leverage

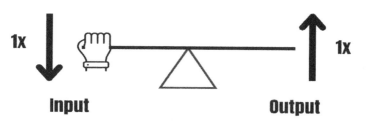

Figure 15

Low Leverage

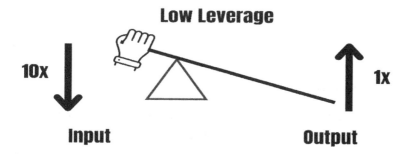

Figure 16

High Leverage

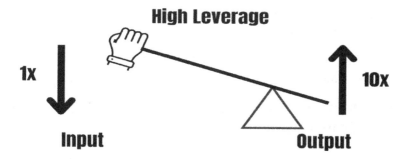

Figure 17

The importance of leverage when it comes to your Master Plan is identifying which activities/outcomes will give you the greatest return on your efforts. In other words, give you the greatest output for your input – figure 17. This lesson is taught very well through Pareto's Law.

Pareto's Law

You may have heard of the 80/20 rule before. This is known as Pareto's Law, which states that 20% of your actions (inputs) will give you 80% of your results (outputs).[17] The other 80% of your actions will only give you the remaining 20% of results. So, the goal is to identify which are the highest leverage activities that will give you the greatest return on investment for your efforts. In other words - identify the 20% high leverage actions.

Examples:

Health and fitness: Goal is to be fit and healthy.

The 20%: Eating healthy, nutritious foods with the correct number of calories, getting the right amount of sleep, drinking quality water and exercising regularly.

The 80%: Supplements, ice baths, stretching, sauna, massages, breathwork, etc.

Startup phase of a business: Goal is to make sales and start building revenue.

The 20%: Marketing, sales and making sure the product you're selling is incredible.

The 80%: The website design, logos, branding, employee compensation plans, etc.

---

[17] Asana, "The Pareto Principle: How the 80/20 Rule Can Help You Be More Effective," *Asana*, accessed September 2, 2024, https://asana.com/resources/pareto-principle-80-20-rule.

Learning to decide which actions make up the 20% is a skill at which you will get better as you start taking action, failing and learning. Also, I'm not saying NEVER do the 80% activities. I'm saying focus on the 20% first. Once finished, move on to the 80% or delegate the 80% when you have the resources to do so.

Tick List vs Outcome

The last lesson to understand before you go through the Master Planning Process, is the difference between an Outcome vs a Tick List. This is the pinnacle of 'mental masturbation' – it's having a big tick list of things you ticked off but might not have achieved anything measurable. Don't get me wrong, you will have things to tick off (20% activities) in order to get the outcome. However, training yourself to focus on achieving the outcome instead of ticking a box will serve you massively.

Here are two examples:

Example One

Outcome: lose 5kg (weight loss)

Tick List:

- Train five times a week (20%) ✓
- Take all my supplements (80%) ✓
- Ice bath (80%) ✓
- Sauna (80%) ✓
- Stretch (80%) ✓
- Meal prep (80%) ✓
- Follow diet plan – calorie deficit – (20%) ✗

Result: You gain 1kg.

Review: You ticked off 6/7 or 85% of your tick list, which might make you feel warm and fuzzy inside. However, you didn't do the biggest 20% action and therefore you did not achieve your result.

Example Two

Outcome: Book in five sales calls (lead generation).

Tick List:

- Send out 100 offers via direct message (20%) ☑
- Clear out emails (80%) ☑
- Post content with a call to action (20%) ☑
- Review KPIs (80%) ☑
- Follow up leads (20%) ☑
- Turned on ads (20%) ☑

Result: Booked in four sales calls.

Review: All your tick list items were completed and more of them were 20% activities. However, the result still wasn't achieved. This gives you the ability to improve what you're doing (you'll learn the Debrief Process at the end of this chapter). You could improve your current activities; you could take out the 80% activities or you could add more 20% activities.

By focusing on the outcome first and the 20% activities to achieve the outcome second , you are able to hold yourself to a high standard, debrief yourself on the results and improve for the future.

The time has come to do the Master Planning Process.

Let's begin.

First, here is the correct flow of goal setting. As you can see in figure 19, you've already ticked off: Purpose, Mission, Vision and Values. Now it's time to dive into the outcomes.

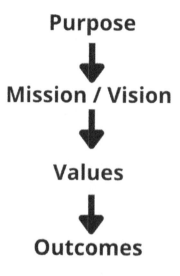

Purpose
⬇
Mission / Vision
⬇
Values
⬇
Outcomes

Figure 19

As you can see in figures 20 and 21, the key is to break down your BHAG (Mission) all the way down into daily action steps. How do you eat a whale in one bite? You can't. You need to cut it into bite-size pieces.

Mission (5-10 years)
⬇
3 Year
⬇
2 Year
⬇
Annual

Figure 20

Annual

Quarterly

Monthly

Weekly

Daily

Figure 21

When you start chunking your goals down, the smaller the goal (daily, weekly, monthly, etc) the more specific it will become. Some goals will be easily chunked down through numbers, and some will need prior goals to be achieved so you can achieve the big goal.

Examples:

Easily chunked down:

Three-year goal: Save $100,000.

Two-year goal: Save $66,666.

One-year goal: Save $33,333

Prior goals needed:

Three-year goal: Open a business.

Two-year goals:

- have lease approved and signed.

- have financing approved for the business.

One-year goals:

- have the business plan finished.

- have a product developed.

There are stepping stones along the way to get to the end result.

The Rules for Master Planning:

- Focus on measurable Outcomes, not Tick List items. (When you get towards weekly and daily goals, your goals will probably become more like Tick List items.)

- Make sure each goal is 'linked' to the next chunked-down goal.

- Only have 3–5 goals for each step.

- Focus on which goals will give you the most leverage towards your Dream Life. (You will get better at determining which goals have more leverage, the more times you do this process.)

- Take your time doing this process, especially steps two and three.

Steps to Complete the Master Planning Process:

1. Review the Purpose, Mission, Vision and Vehicle. Write down your Mission in the 'Mission Statement' section.

2. Brainstorm 10–15 ideas of what you believe needs to be achieved within the next three years to move towards the Mission.

3. Decide which top three to five outcomes will give you the most leverage to move towards the Mission. Write those outcomes down in the 'Three-Year Goals' section.

4. Chunk your three-year goals down to two-year goals and put those goals into the 'Two-Year Goals' section.

5. Chunk those two-year goals into 12-month goals and put those into the '12-Month Goals' section.

6. Chunk those 12-month goals into quarterly (90-day) goals and put them into the 'Quarterly Goals' section.

7. Chunk those quarterly goals into monthly goals and put them into the 'Monthly Goals' section.

8. Chunk those monthly goals into weekly goals and put them into the 'Weekly Goals' section.

9. Chunk those weekly goals into daily outcomes/activities and put them into the 'Daily Huddle' section. The huddle structure will be explained soon.

This possibly can seem overwhelming, but once you go through the process you'll understand how simple and how powerful this process is. If you go to page 262 here is my entire current Life Master Plan to give you an idea of how this works.

The initial steps to the planning process are on the following pages. However, from Step Three onwards, write your answers on page 269 in your Master Plan template.

(Hot tip: Complete the first version of the planning process on some spare paper to allow for mistakes, then put the final version into The Master Plan template.):

Step 1: Review the Purpose, Mission, Vision and Vehicle. Write down your Mission into the 'Mission Statement' section on page 269 (you have probably done this already).

Step 2: Brainstorm 10–15 ideas of what you believe needs to be achieved within the next three years to move towards the Mission:

1. _____

2. _____

3. _____

4. _____

5. _____

6. _____

7. _____

8. _____

9. _____

10. _____

11. _____

12. _____

13. _____

14. _____

15. _____

Step 3: Decide which top 3–5 outcomes will give you the most leverage to move towards the Mission. Write those outcomes down in the 'Three-Year Goals' section on page 269.

Step 4: Chunk your three-year goals down to two-year goals and put those goals into the '2-Year Goals' section on page 269.

Step 5: Chunk those two-year goals into 12-Month goals and put those goals into the '12-Month Goals' section on page 269.

Step 6: Chunk those 12 -month goals into quarterly (90-day) goals and put those goals into the 'Quarterly Goals' section on page 270

Step 7: Chunk those quarterly goals into monthly goals and put those goals into the 'Monthly Goals' section on page 270.

Step 8: Chunk those monthly goals into weekly goals and put those goals into the 'Weekly Goals' section on page 270.

Step 9: Chunk those weekly goals into daily outcomes/activities and put those into the 'Daily Huddle' section, into 'What are your outcomes to be completed today?' on page 271.

Congrats! You've completed the Master Planning Process. You now know your Life's Purpose and Mission and what you need to do today to move towards it. Pretty cool, right? But we've got three small steps to wrap up.

Debrief Process

The U.S. Air Force has a remarkable 98% completion rate of its Missions.[18] Compare that to the 90% of businesses that fail. So why does the air force execute at such a high percentage? There are many answers, but one reason is that it has a debriefing process. *"The focus of the debrief is to identify and communicate what happened, why it happened, discuss how we can do it better next time, and finally determine if we met our objectives."*[19] This is a simple yet powerful tool to use with your goal setting (and in any performance environment). Here is how the process works:

Step 1: What is the outcome/objective we want to achieve? Have a very clear and measurable outcome with a plan of action.

– Answer the following once the plan has been completed –

Step 2: Was the outcome/objective achieved? Yes or no? Gives accountability and transparency.

Step 3:

---

[18] Karl J. Veit, "Focus Yiels 98 Percent Mission Capable Rate," *U.S. Air Force*, last modified December 12, 2003, https://www.af.mil/News/Article-Display/Article/139303/focus-yields-98-percent-mission-capable-rate/.

[19] Dan Hawkins, "The Art of the Debrief," *Air Education and Training Command (AETC)*, U.S. Air Force, last modified July 24, 2019, https://www.aetc.af.mil/News/Article-Display/Article/1917581/the-art-of-the-debrief/.

a) **If yes: Why was this achieved?** Gives feedback to what worked well.

b) **If no: Why was this not achieved?** Gives feedback to what didn't work well.

Step 4: What can you do to improve for next time? Allows you to grow and improve for next time.

It's simple, effective and easy to follow. You'll see the word *debrief* show up in the Huddle Structure and Review Process. When you see the word *debrief*, you now know what it means.

The Huddle Structure

Effective high-performing teams – business, sports, military, etc. – have regular check-ins (Huddles) to connect, debrief and discuss any important topics. Think of a football team – once the team scores or gets scored against, the team comes together to regroup, assess what happened and refocus to move forward. These are some of the reasons to follow the Daily Huddle Structure. Here are the steps and why we do each of them:

Step 1: What are you excited about today? This builds excitement for the day ahead.

Step 2: What were your outcomes for last week and were they done or not done? Why or why not? Debrief, to create accountability and transparency. This step is done only once a week, usually on a Monday morning or on whatever day you start your week.

Step 3: What were your outcomes for yesterday and were they done or not done? Why or why not? Debrief, to create accountability and transparency.

Step 4: What are your outcomes to be completed today? Gives clarity to execute on the day and continues the accountability and transparency.

Step 5: Do you require any support from anyone to complete these outcomes today? This removes any excuse for the following day about why these outcomes could not be completed.

Step 6: What are you grateful for today? This builds good energy for yourself and a team if this is done within a team environment, plus all the other benefits that gratitude offers.

(Side note for huddles: Depending how you work and what days you work, the structure will change slightly. Some people work every day of the week, some don't and that's okay.)

(Hot Tip: If you work as part of a team or have your own team, get the entire team involved in Daily Huddles. Once you're in flow, a Daily Huddle takes only about 90 seconds to complete per person. That investment of time is worth its weight in gold in productivity. If you work for someone else, I'd still recommend doing your own personal huddle, but in this case huddle with an accountability buddy.)

The last step is to know how and when to review The Master Plan.

The Review Process

The Review Process allows you to refine, innovate and adjust The Master Plan. As you follow your Master Plan, you will grow, you will gain more skills, resources and knowledge. The world you live in will also change massively. Depending on when you're reading this, the world will look a lot different than it was when I wrote these words, so it is important to refine your plan constantly.

Here are the rhythms of reviewing and refining your Master Plan:

Annually/Quarterly:

Review, debrief and rewrite everything: Purpose, Mission, Vision, Values and all outcomes (The Master Plan).

Monthly: Eight times a year (the Annual and Quarterlies take up the other four):

Review everything: Purpose, Mission, Vision, Values and all outcomes (The Master Plan). Debrief and rewrite monthly and weekly outcomes.

Weekly: 52 times a year:

Review everything: Purpose, Mission, Vision, Values and all outcomes (The Master Plan). Debrief and rewrite weekly outcomes.

There you have it, a step-by-step process of taking your Purpose and breaking it all the way down into daily actionable steps. This can seem overwhelming if you haven't been completing the process as we went through it. After you've finished the entire process once, it's really simple and easy to refine.

Real-Life Example

The power of this exact process allowed my mentor to increase his business tenfold and me to triple my business within a year. Here's how:

Let me take you back to about three years into the gym chapter of my journey. When I had become a gym owner at age 20 my mentor, Scott, had become my business partner after selling half of the gym to me. We had been hustling our asses off for the past three years and we had one successful gym to show for it. We thought that wasn't a bad achievement. However, every day was chaotic and very unstructured. We were making moment-to-moment decisions, based solely on what we thought would be effective, and those decisions were heavily influenced by our emotions:

"Let's do a marketing giveaway this month!"

"Let's change the workouts and make them different!"

"Let's get a DJ to play at the gym to make the vibes better!"

"Let's paint the walls a different colour to make the gym look better!"

"Let's run a 12-week challenge!"

"Let's buy more equipment for the gym!"

"Let's hire more trainers!"

"Let's run Facebook ads!"

"Let's buy a body scanner for the gym!"

"Let's move the gym to a bigger building!"

These were the day-to-day conversations we were having. Some of the ideas were good, some were terrible. Some were the right decisions to be made, but just not the right timing. We were like two excited kids with ADHD, who would think of an idea that looked like a good decision and would go all in on it. That worked for a while, but eventually we hit a wall. We had the one gym that was doing well, but the growth had stopped. Something had to change.

Scott had heard of a seminar from an Australian entrepreneur who helps business owners scale their enterprise. Scott grabbed tickets for both of us, and when we attended a four-day business boot camp, it absolutely blew our minds with what we didn't know. We went through leadership, sales, marketing, legalities, organisational charts, operations, planning and so much more. We got so much information from the boot camp, but we had so many more questions about how to execute it all.

At the end of the four days, as always, there was a sales pitch making a bigger offer, which in this case was a 12-month Mastermind program. The entrepreneur showed a lot of testimonials from business owners who talked about tripling their revenue/income or increasing it up to twenty times whilst reducing the time they worked in their businesses.

We were so committed to growing our business that we decided we would do anything to join this Mastermind. We had the initial conversation with the sales rep about potentially joining and we were just waiting to hear the cost. When he told us, our jaws dropped. $44,000 for the twelve months. I've never spent that much money on anything in my life. That was more than a full-time salary at the time. The business was profitable, but not enough to cover that kind of extra expense. But we knew we needed the help, so we agreed to it anyway. We put down a deposit making us committed to the decision, and we knew we would figure out how to pay for it. We could barely afford the repayments, in truth, but by making extra sales at the gym, borrowing money and minimising our personal expenses, we were able to make it happen.

The following year was life-changing for us. The biggest shift was in planning – actually breaking down what our Mission was and building a tactical plan to execute it. Planning sounded so simple, but it was something we just weren't doing. When we finally went through the planning process (similar to the one you just completed) we came away with so much clarity. It was time to execute.

Within 12 months of learning the planning process, I was able to open my second gym whilst tripling the revenue. Within the year, Scott had opened 10 franchised gyms.

Let's refresh:

- Three years without any planning = one gym. Scott and Lewis.

- 12 months with high-quality planning = 10 gyms. Scott.

- 12 months with high-quality planning = two gyms and tripling the revenue. Lewis.

- Increasing his business ten-fold within 12 months. Scott.

- Tripling his business within 12 months. Lewis.

Not bad. Why did this happen? Instead of taking random actions (working on the 80%) we both got clear on the most important actions that were needed (the 20%). In other words, we figured out what the high leverage activities were for us to act on.

Quick status update:

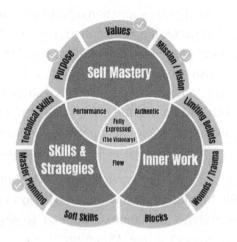

Figure 22

Summary of Master Planning:

1. Chunk down your Mission, all the way down to daily actionable outcomes.

2. Focus your attention and resources on the high leverage activities (the 20%).

3. Follow the meeting rhythms to make sure you're adjusting and staying on the right path towards your Mission.

You're crushing it! It's almost time to move into the Inner Work pillar of *The Inspired Life Method*. Before we do that, I want to give you a simple but really powerful tool to help you to never lack motivation again.

Have you ever had goals that you actually wanted to achieve but you had to do things you didn't want to do? And because you didn't want to do those things, you procrastinated or even gave up on those goals? I'm certainly guilty of this. To help you overcome these problems, which are guaranteed to show up for you, you're about to learn how to program your mind to WANT to do ANYTHING. Big call I know but let me show you in the next chapter.

CHAPTER 8

Unlimited Motivation

*"The need for motivation is a
symptom of an uninspired goal."*
                                    – Lewis Huckstep

I am killing myself personally, because I don't know any better. I sit down at the desk in the office of one of my gyms. It's 7pm, I've been awake since 4.30am, and I have worked all day with one 30-minute nap. I've eaten delicious but unhealthy processed lunch from the food truck that comes around. I'm exhausted. I can barely keep my eyes open but, fuelled by my feeling of not being enough and trying to overcompensate through overachieving, I push on to finish doing more work for the business. I finish my work by 10.30pm and drive home, calling into McDonald's on the way. Once home, I quickly jump into bed to get some sleep, but then wake up and repeat the hustle saga all over again.

This was my life for about five years. I did it all to maximise how much time I could work and how I could spend as little as possible. I had tunnel Vision in an unhealthy extreme way. My health and fitness were the worst they'd ever been, which was so ironic for someone who owned gyms. To get attention back then, I had to show the world how tough and hard-working I was. Here's a screenshot I found from that stage of my life:

Figure 23

Most nights the 6.30pm gym class would be a quieter class, consisting of never more than five people. The trainer often popped her head into my dungeon (office) and asked if I'd like to jump in and do the workout with the clients. My go-to response would be, "*No, I have more work that I need to do.*" This happened at least three or four times a week. I would always neglect my health because I would rather work more on the business. I genuinely wanted to be healthier, but every time the opportunity popped up, I made excuses to do something else.

This was before I learned about Values, Purpose, Mission and Vision (and the Inner Work you'll be doing soon). I didn't understand why I kept making excuses and procrastinating about things I genuinely wanted to do. Then I figured it out. I attended yet another seminar (self-development junkie that I am) where we went through Values (the style of Values in Chapter 2), and we went through the topic of motivation. The teacher explained: "The only reason that you do or do not do something is because there are more benefits to the thing that you choose, in relation to your highest Values."

Let's use an example:

If you choose to hit the snooze button and go back to bed, instead of getting up and going to the gym, in that moment of decision there are more benefits by hitting the snooze button:

- You get to stay warm.

- You don't have to feel the pain of training.

- You get to cuddle your partner for longer.

- You get more sleep.

- Etc.

On the other hand, if you decide to get up and go to the gym, in that moment of decision, there are more benefits to going to the gym:

- You will have a good mindset for the day.

- You will feel confident and strong physically.

- You get to meet your friends at the gym.

- You set a great example for your children.

- Etc.

Every decision you make is filtered through 'Which has more benefits?' and especially 'Which has more benefits to your highest Values.' So, the exercise I was given was to write down 200 benefits to my top three Values, in relation to doing the thing I am wanting to be better at (or that I want to stop doing). No, that isn't a typo – 200 is correct.

I wanted to be healthier, so I wrote down my top three Values, which at the time were Coaching, Learning and Business. I started listing 200 benefits of how my top three Values would improve by looking after my health more. The first 20 were relatively easy, but after that it was challenging. One by one though, I kept finding more as I asked myself two magic questions (you'll learn them soon) and the benefits kept coming. By the end of the exercise, which took me 30 minutes to complete, I WANTED to be better with my health because I saw how it would allow me to fulfil my Values at a higher level.

Since that day, I have consistently looked after my health, trained four to seven times a week, eaten healthier (still love some naughty food from time to time) and I've never needed 'motivation' to do it. Why? Because I had intrinsic inspiration to WANT to do it.

Here's a really quick story to understand this even more.

I have had many parents come to the gyms over the years and this tool made it so easy to help them decide if they wanted to join. Many would commonly say, "I'm just not a motivated person." To that I would respond, "Bullshit, you're just not motivated to go to the gym and that's okay. You said you're a parent. Do you need motivation to spend time with your kids?" They would commonly answer, "No, I love spending time with my kids." The parent had a high Value on family and a low Value on health. Then my magic question, "How will you be a better parent by looking after your health more?"

I was getting them to link benefits to their health (a low Value) to their time with their children (a high Value). That's the tool in its simplest form. Let's do it now.

Linking Benefits

As you just heard from those two real-life experiences, if you require motivation to do something, it simply means that you don't see enough benefits to do that thing as it relates to your highest Values. Think about yourself right now. You're reading this book; no-one is forcing you to read. At some level you WANT to be reading this book. And by reading this book you believe it will help you with your Values at some level. Am I right?

128

So how do we use this information? Great question. As with my own story, for anything that you need to do within your plan to create a Dream Life – but that you <u>don't want</u> to do – just link the benefits of doing that thing to your top three Values. Yes, it's literally that simple.

(<u>Side note</u>: Once you have more resources, the goal is to delegate the things you're not inspired to do to people who are inspired to do them, but keep in mind that some things can't be delegated, such as your health.)

Steps for Linking Benefits:

1. List your top three Values.

2. List the specific actions you want to start doing or be better at.

3. Write down many benefits (200 is recommended, around 66 for each Value) to how your top three Values will improve, by doing those specific actions.

4. Use the two magic questions when you get stuck:

    a. If there was one more, what would it be?

    b. What's a benefit of that benefit?

Here's an example of the second magic question being used:

Values: Family, business, travel.

Specific action: Going to the gym.

Question: How will my family benefit from me going to the gym more?

Benefit: My mindset will be better because training improves it, so I'll have more energy and be a better version of myself for my family.

What's a benefit of that benefit? Because I will have more energy for my family, I'll be able to build deeper and stronger relationships with them.

What's a benefit of that benefit? Because I will have deeper and stronger relationships with my family, I will be a happier person overall.

What's a benefit of that benefit? Because I'll be a happier person overall, I'll show up as a better leader for my business.

What's a benefit of that benefit? Because I'll show up as a better leader for my business, the business will grow more and make more money.

What's a benefit of that benefit? Because I'll be making more money, I can go traveling with my family.

You get the idea. There's literally endless amounts of benefits. Simple. Let's do it.

Specific Actions:	#1 Value:	#2 Value:	#3 Value:
#1 Action:	How does this action benefit #1 Value?	How does this action benefit #2 Value?	How does this action benefit #3 Value?

(See over the page for steps to complete this table – TABLE 4)

Step 1: Write down your top three Values into TABLE 4

Step 2: Write the number one specific action you want to start doing or be better at into the table.

Step 3: Write the benefits (200 is recommended) into the table to see how your top three Values will improve by doing those specific actions.

Step 4: Use the magic questions when you hit a mental block. There are always more benefits.

(Top tip - The benefits can cross over Values. Example: a benefit for Value #1 will then benefit Value #2. Doing this makes this exercise a lot easier.)

Estimated time to complete TABLE 4: 20 minutes

You can now wire your mind to WANT to do anything. It's literally rewiring your mind to do things that will help you to create your Dream Life. Pretty crazy stuff. You can also do the reverse of this exercise:

Link drawbacks to your top three Values by doing an action.

Example: What is a drawback to my family (Value) by me smoking (action)?

Summary of Unlimited Motivation:

1. We only do things that we perceive have more benefits to our highest Values.

2. Whatever you want to be better at, just link benefits to your top three Values.

3. You can wire your mind to do anything or to stop doing anything.

It's now time to move into the Inner Healing pillar. This is my favourite pillar. Strap in.

CHAPTER 9

Inner Healing

"Trauma is not what happens to you,
it's what happens inside of you."

– Gabor Maté.[20]

"Open this fucking door you little cunt. You don't fucking talk like that to me in my house." I'll never forget those words.

Lying in my bed, hearing the anger in my dad's voice start to build, my whole body starts to shake in fear of what might happen next. I can hear my older brother's voice in the argument going back and forth with my dad. The insults are getting more hurtful and personal. My body is filled with anxiety, my mind is filled with fear. I lock my door to try to protect myself from any potential pain that will come.

Although this feeling of fear and anxiety was quite common in my upbringing, my nervous system still got overloaded every time there was mental, emotional or physical violence around.

As the argument continues, I hear a loud, violent scream: *"Come here you, little fucking shit!"* This is followed by the sound of my brother's footsteps running down the hallway and then a massive slam of his bedroom door. *He made it to his room in time, he's safe* ...or so I think.

My body is shaking with fear and my mind racing over what might happen to my brother and maybe to me. The only little peace of mind I

---

[20] Gabor Maté, "The Wisdom of Trauma," *Dr. Gabor Maté*, accessed September 2, 2024, https://drgaborrmate.com/the-wisdom-of-trauma/.

feel is that my door is locked, and by the sound of things, my brother's is as well. Within three seconds of hearing my brother's door slam shut. I hear aggressive banging and yelling.

BANG BANG BANG

"Open this fucking door, you little cunt. You don't fucking talk like that to me in my house!"

As it was quite common in my household, I thought this would be the usual peak of the event and that eventually Dad would calm back down. No, not this time. The noises to come were etched into my mind that day.

The loud banging from before got even louder and it turned into crashing, ripping and tearing noises. I was too scared to leave my bedroom to see what was happening, but from what I could hear, my dad was breaking down my brother's door. I started to go into an extremely heightened state of anxiety.

My heart was pounding. My body was shaking. Then suddenly, my mind went blank. My memory of what happened after that moment is gone. I have completely dissociated from the event to protect myself. I remember later on in the night, when I sneaked out to go to the bathroom, seeing my brother's door shattered all over the floor. My brother wasn't in his room.

Where is he? What happened? Did my dad hurt him? Am I next? All of these thoughts were racing through my head. It took 17 more years for me to ask my brother about that night. When I did, he said he had very few memories of it. *"That was just how it was for us growing up and it was just normal,"* he reminded me.

That event was one of the countless experiences I had when I was younger that created trauma within me. Although those experiences were so overwhelming, painful and challenging at the time, once healed, they actually gave me the strengths I have to day.

You're about to learn the role that trauma and 'Inner Work' play, and how your unhealed trauma is the invisible puppet master controlling your life. You'll learn how anyone can heal trauma by doing Inner Work, and how your trauma is your greatest gift once you've healed it. Once you understand the concept of Inner Work, you'll actually be using three tools that I've created in the coming chapters to start or continue your healing journey.

To demonstrate how to turn your pain into purpose and your wounds into wisdom, I will be sharing how I used the second tool in this book to go through and heal that specific traumatic memory.

Disclaimer:

Before I start this section on Inner Work/healing/trauma I want to make this very clear. I am not a traditionally qualified therapist, counsellor, psychologist or psychotherapist, nor do I have any other traditional qualifications in this area. I have, however, studied and have been trained in numerous healing modalities (you'll see them soon). I have consciously been on my healing journey for the past 10 years, and have coached more than 4000 people to heal and evolve. What I am sharing is based only on my personal healing experiences, as well as those of my clients, and from the knowledge I've gained from studying some of the greatest minds on this planet, past and present. If you do not feel comfortable doing any of the following processes provided in the coming chapters, please do not complete them.

Of all the topics that we'll be covering on our journey together, this one is the deepest and has the most controversy to it. There are thousands of books that talk about aspects of Inner Work. From Carl Jung, Sigmund Freud, Joe Dispenza, John Demartini, Tony Robbins, Wayne Dyer, Lousie Hay, Gabor Maté, Nicole Lepera, Bessel Van Der Kolk, Bruce Lipton, Sarah Woodhouse, Ken Wilber, Cody McAuliffe and David Hawkins, and so many others. These are just some of the healers and teachers who have made an impact on millions of lives, including my own.

What Is Inner Work?

I have seen many definitions of Inner Work. This is the one that I think puts it the best: *'The psychological (also emotional, physical and spiritual) practice of identifying and dissolving the contractions and blockages that obscure your Inner Light (True Authentic Self) for the purposes of self-awareness, healing, transformation and expansion."*[21]

If I were to put it in an even simpler way:

"To dissolve/heal the wounds and blockages that are masking your true self."

Inner Work is the journey of healing/processing/integrating/ loving all aspects of who you are. (I will be using these words interchangeably in the coming chapters.) The good. The bad. The ugly. The shame. The fear. The guilt. The grief. EVERYTHING. Doing Inner Work allows you to express your true self more. There are also many other benefits that you'll soon see.

For easier communication, instead of using all the different words to describe things that go into Inner Work such as: trauma, mental blocks, limiting beliefs, shadows, emotional scars, emotional baggage, inner turmoil, wounds, etc., when broadly describing Inner Work, I will be using the words heal or healing and wound or wounds. Yes, the word *wounds* can represent quite different things when it comes to Inner Work, so when being more specific I will use the specific words.

Why Is It Important to Do Inner Work?

You read earlier about Pareto's Law, the 80/20 rule. It has been said and researched that: 'Success in life is 80% psychology (mindset) and 20% mechanics (skills)'. This means that if you don't have the right mindset to follow through with your goals (Master Plan) and do

---

[21] Mateo Sol, "Inner Work: A Guide to Inner Child Healing and Shadow Work," *LonerWolf*, last modified February 10, 2023, https://lonerwolf.com/inner-work/#h-what-is-inner-work.

whatever it takes to be successful, then it doesn't matter how great your skills/strategies are.

Let's use health as an example. Is the skillset needed to be relatively healthy so complicated that most people will never figure it out? Absolutely not. Train regularly, eat as much healthy, unprocessed food as possible, make sure your calories and macro nutrients are in the right range for your goal, drink water and get quality sleep. It's actually very simple. You can find the answers on YouTube or Google. Then why is most of the world's population unhealthy? In Australia in 2022, almost two-thirds (65.8%) of adults were overweight or obese.[22] Why? Because most people don't have the mindset needed to find the strategy and/or follow through with the strategy. This is why this book focuses mainly on the mindset (Self-Mastery and Inner Work) with a little bit of the skills (selecting the Right Vehicle and Master Planning).

Your 'wounds' (traumas, limiting beliefs and blocks) that you haven't worked through yet are directly influencing your mindset. They will also continue to 'trigger you' and cause you to self-sabotage until you heal them. Your coping mechanisms from your unhealed wounds are the invisible puppet masters controlling your actions and therefore, unconsciously, your life.

How Do You Do Inner Work?

The paraphrased quote that allows me to explain how to do Inner Work the best comes from martial artist Bruce Lee: *"There is no ultimate martial art, but only the ultimate martial artist, who knows all martial arts and knows when to pull from the right one at the right time to get the right result."* In the context of healing, this is saying that there is no

---

[22] Australian Bureau of Statistics, "Waist Circumference and BMI," *Australia Bureau of Statistics,* last modified May 24, 2023,
https://www.abs.gov.au/statistics/health/health-conditions-and-risks/waist-circumference-and-bmi/latest-release#:~:text=Over%20the%20last%20decade%2C%20the,31.7%25%20over%20the%20same%20period.

ultimate way to heal. In fact, there are dozens if not hundreds of ways/modalities in which to heal, I'll be giving you a list of heaps soon. All modalities have their different focuses and will work on different 'bodies', which you can see in Figure 24. Knowing what body your wounds are in will allow you to use the right modality to get the transformation you're seeking.

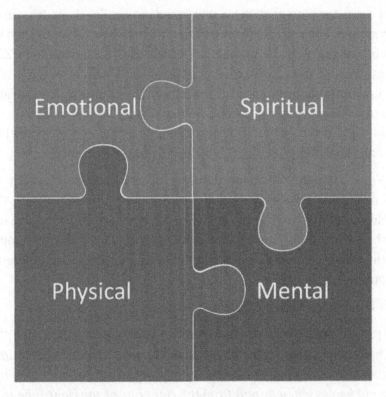

Figure 24. The 'four bodies' visual model by Cody McAuliffe

Figure 24 shows you the four bodies that have to be healed in order to heal in an integrated and complete way. Most people get stuck in one modality to heal, because it may have helped them at the start of their journey. To continue to deepen and 'complete' your healing journey, you must integrate the other bodies.

Mental body: Our thoughts, memories, perceptions, attitudes, beliefs, limiting beliefs and judgements. In other words, our Ego.

Physical Body (somatic): Our skin and everything under the skin, the brain and everything between the ears. It is the skeletal system, organs, blood, veins and ligaments.

Emotional Body: The nervous system, hormones, water and water release (tears).

Spiritual Body: Connection to all things, including the earth/self, to what we call God, the universe, the beyond, the divine or higher self. It connects us to all that is.

(Side note: I'm aware of a fifth body, the energetic body. I've also been taught from different healers that there are up to 14 bodies to heal. Due to the level of complexity and my current level of awareness/knowledge, we will be sticking to the four bodies for the rest of this book.)

You will have wounds/blocks/limitations in all of the four bodies. But you will have more in some bodies depending on your upbringing, your parents, your biochemical makeup, your past lives (if you believe in them) and many other factors. The important thing is to integrate all of them over time.

We could dive into each body in so much detail that each would require its own book, and there are already plenty of books that expand on these in a lot more depth. For your understanding, just know that there are many ways to heal.

Remember that you're never 100% healed. We are on a lifelong healing journey, forever becoming more healed but never completely healed, just like an exponential graph where the line never touches the x-axis. (See fig. 25)

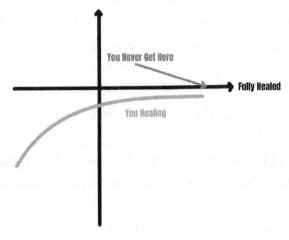

Figure 25

Cleaning up, Growing up, Waking up and Showing up

Now, to be able to heal within the four bodies there are four 'ways' of healing. Ken Wilber in his book *Integral Theory* talks about the four 'Ups'.[23]

---

[23] Dustin DiPerna, "Integral Theory and the Future of Religion," *Integral World*, accessed September 2, 2024, https://www.integralworld.net/diperna06.html.

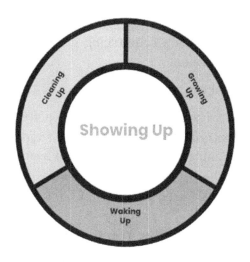

Figure 26

<u>Waking up</u>: Different stages of consciousness. This involves transcending the Ego (we'll learn about the Ego later in this chapter) and recognising the interconnectedness of all things. Think of the difference in awareness and consciousness about reality to a baby, to a child, to a teenager and to an adult.

<u>Growing up</u>: Developmental growth and maturation. This evolves through various stages of cognitive, emotional and moral development. Growing up involves the gaining of skills, knowledge and wisdom necessary for navigating life's challenges. Think of the difference in maturity and knowledge of a baby, of a child, of a teenager and of an adult.

<u>Cleaning up</u>: The process of healing and integrating unresolved mental and emotional wounds. It entails addressing past traumas, shadow aspects, or limiting beliefs (and other things) that may be hindering personal growth and well-being.

<u>Showing up</u>: The importance of actively engaging with life and making meaningful contributions to the world. It involves living

authentically, aligned with one's Values and Purpose, and having a positive impact on others and the world. Showing up may involve taking action, serving others or pursuing goals that align with one's Purpose, Mission and Values.

The important takeaway from this:

Make sure you're leaning into all four 'Ups' in your healing journey. The three tools that you'll be going through soon are Growing Up, Cleaning Up and Waking Up tools. You've also been empowered with the ability of Showing Up more, by being aware of everything we've covered so far – Values, Purpose, Mission, Vision, etc.

Modalities/Tools That Allow You to Heal and Do Inner Work

I have been on my healing journey (consciously) for more than 10 years, which is still very new in my opinion. I have experience as a client and been certified in just a few of the many different modalities/tools there are out there. I'm going to give you a list of all the modalities I have:

1. Experienced as a client.

2. Been certified in.

3. Been made aware of but have yet to experience.

I will also put next to each modality which body that I believe it heals through, from the ones I've personally experienced. I may be off or incorrect because I haven't experienced all of them. And please keep in mind that some modalities touch on more than just one body.

Key:

If I've experienced the modality as a client = *

I have been certified in the modality = <u>underlined.</u>

Which body: Physical = (P) Emotional = (E) Mental = (M) Spiritual = (S).

The list:

- <u>Ego Dissolving*</u> – my own technique that you're going to be doing in this book. (M, E)

- <u>Balancing Process*</u> – my own technique that you're going to be doing in this book. (M, E)

- <u>Meditation*</u> – different styles of meditation touch different bodies. You will be given two styles of meditation in this book. (P, E, M, S)

- <u>NLP: Neuro Linguistic Programming*</u> (M, E)

- <u>Timeline therapy*</u> (M, E)

- <u>Hypnotherapy*</u> (M, E)

- <u>Negative Emotional Release Techniques*</u> (M, E)

- <u>Demartini facilitator*</u> (M)

- <u>Breathwork*</u> (P, E, S) – different types of breathwork touch different bodies

- <u>Holographic transformation*</u> (P, E, M, S)

- Reiki healing* (E)

- Sound healing* (E)

- Plant medicine – Psilocybin mushrooms, Rapé and Ayahuasca*. There are many more medicines (P, E, M, S)

- Journalling* (M)

- Crystal healing* (E)

- Massage therapy* (P, E)

- Inner child healing* (E, M)

- Shadow work* (E, M,)

- Astrology healing*(E, S)

- Chakra clearing* (E, S)

- Yoga* (P, E)

- Ecstatic dancing* (P, E)

- Primal screaming* (P, E)

- Tantric healing* (P, E)

- Shame Circles* – being seen in your shame (often these are done while being naked) (M, E)

- Traditional therapy* – there are many versions such as talk therapy, family therapy, group therapy, etc.

- Kahuna massage – traditional Hawaiian massage * (P, E)

- Human design

- Psychotherapy

- Quantum energy healing

- Acupuncture

- Reflexology

- Cognitive Behavioural Therapy – CBT

- Emotional Freedom Technique – EFT/Tapping

- Akashic healing

- Womb healing

- Eye movement desensitisation and reprocessing – EMDR

- Internal family systems

- Kinesiology

- Human design

- Psych-K

- Feng Shui

- Past life regression therapy

- Family constellation therapy

- Angelic healing

- Emotion code therapy

- Aroma freedom technique

- Theta healing

- Chi Nei Tsang

- Integrated energy therapy – IET

- Kundalini activation process – KAP

- Somatic movement

I guarantee that I have missed out many other modalities, but as you can see, there are many, many ways for you to do your Inner Work. Different modalities work better for different people, depending on who you are and in which of your bodies your wounds lie. My invitation to you is to try as many as you can. I'm on a quest to experience as many modalities as I can and to be certified in the ones with which I align most (like becoming the ultimate martial artist). In this book I will be giving you three tools to start or continue your healing journey. (I also offer many more tools with my other services.)

Here are my three rules when looking for who to work with as a healer/therapist:

1. **You feel safe in their space/presence**. To heal, you must be able to be vulnerable. However, the Ego will avoid pain (you'll learn about this soon), so it will shut down and put the walls up if it doesn't feel safe. Even if the healer you're wanting to work with has the best tools to help you, if you don't feel safe in their presence, find someone else.

2. **They are actively 'doing their own work'.** You wouldn't listen to a personal trainer who is unhealthy, so why would you listen to someone on how to heal, if they aren't doing their own healing? If the person you're wanting to work with isn't embodying what they teach, I'd find someone else. There's a big difference between knowing and embodying.

3. **They have proven results for other clients.** Ultimately that's what you're paying them for. If they haven't gotten results with others, I'd be looking elsewhere.

Summary of Inner Work:

1. Success in anything in life is 80% mindset.

2. Your Inner Work (or lack thereof) directly influences (creates) your mindset.

3. Until you heal your 'wounds' you will continue to be triggered and self-sabotage your goals (life).

4. There are four bodies in the context of this book through which to heal – mental, emotional, physical and spiritual.

5. There are four 'ups' (ways) to use to heal – cleaning up, growing up, waking up and showing up.

6. There are dozens, if not hundreds, of modalities to heal.

7. You are never fully healed, there is always more to do.

8. The more you heal, the more authentic and expressed you become.

Okay, you now have a solid foundation of understanding Inner Work. But how do you apply this in real life? Great question. By being aware of your triggers, your traumatic reactions, you will be able to identify your wounds (trauma), then you can use whatever modality is necessary (based on what body it's in) to heal through it.

Trauma, Traumatic Reactions, Triggers

> *"The degree that you resist reality,*
> *is the degree that you suffer."*
>
> *"Past hurt informs future fear."*
>
> **– Peter Crone**

I instantly triggered her. I revealed a wound in her ...

I've just finished a busy day of work. Being the usual chef in the relationship, I start walking towards the kitchen to start the nightly dinner cooking routine. My beautiful partner, who normally is the receiver of my cooking, surprisingly asks me, "Baby, would you like me to cook you dinner?" "Absolutely," I respond with a big smile. Instead, I make my way to the living room to start looking for a movie to watch.

I hear her voice coming from the kitchen, "Do you want an egg on your burger?" "Hell yes, I'd love one," I respond. I'm getting really excited for my juicy burger at this point. Once I've picked which movie to watch (it's a Marvel movie, obviously), I decide to go and check on the status of my burger.

As I walk into the kitchen, the first thing I check on is the egg. To my surprise, what I expect to be a fried egg (given it is to go in a burger), looks like a bad attempt at scrambled eggs. Out of confusion and in a friendly way, I ask my partner, "Babe, what's happened to the egg?" Instantly, I feel and see a massive shift in her. Her face changes from neutral to hurt and her energy instantly becomes really tense. I have triggered her.

"GET OUT OF THE KITCHEN!" she yells. "I can't do anything good enough for you!" The words and the energy she is sharing is that of a hurt, young girl. I have revealed an unhealed wound in my partner. In situations like this, my partner and I go through what we call a *'healing conversation'* by regulating our emotions, giving each other space or (not in this instance but sometimes) just fighting through it.

Once the storm passes and we have both regulated our emotions back to neutral, we sit on the couch (with our burgers), to reconnect and discuss what was brought to the surface. "What did I trigger in you?" I ask. She knows straight away what it is. "Growing up, all the male figures around me would say that everything I did wasn't enough. If I made dinner, it wasn't good enough. If I sang, they'd tell me to shut up. If I tried to do any form of sports, I wasn't athletic enough. My exes would comment on how I was not beautiful or sexy enough. I just wanted to make you a beautiful meal, and it came across that I wasn't enough."

Whenever you get triggered, it's revealing an unhealed wound inside you but, with this awareness, you'll be able to use a tool or modality to go and heal through it.

I thanked my partner for being so strong and vulnerable and for having the healing conversation with me. I finished with this question, "Do you have the tools needed for you to heal through this and are you committed to healing through this, so it doesn't get triggered again?"

"I do. Thank you for helping me through this," she replied.

Sometimes these tough (healing) conversations can blow up, but 100% of the time we're able to come to a resolution like this because of the tools and awareness we have – the same tools you're learning in this book. And yes, the burger did taste delicious. "Thank you, baby."

Be Aware of the Signs the Universe Is Sending

> *"Nothing triggers you – it reveals what's inside of you."*
> – Lewis Huckstep

A book that really helped me with the understanding of how to do Inner Work/healing practically is: *You're Not Broken – Break Free from Trauma and Reclaim Your Life* by Dr Sarah Woodhouse, a psychologist and trauma expert. These are my biggest takeaways and how you can use them to heal:

1. **Trauma (wound) is unprocessed memories**. This simple sentence really hit me and makes so much sense. I would add and reframe this line to: **Trauma is unprocessed experiences**. This is because memories are part of the <u>Mental Body</u> that we spoke about earlier. But what if the trauma is precognitive? This means that the trauma was earlier than you have memories of, probably before the age of three years – including in the womb and trauma passed down genetically through your family. That means the trauma is going to be in one of the other three bodies, which requires a different modality for healing.

2. **Trauma, traumatic reactions and triggers**.

   a. **Trauma**: This is the event that we go through and experience. The formula Dr Woodhouse uses is: Traumatic experience = perceived threat + overwhelm + powerlessness. I would also add to this, especially when you're younger, your needs not being met: not being seen, being heard, being held, being validated and being loved.

   b. **Traumatic Reactions**: This is how you reacted when the trauma happened. This can be called coping mechanisms/strategies and also shadows (shadow work).

   Here's what traumatic reactions can look like:

   - The knot in your stomach when you see someone.

   - Shame/anger (other negative emotions) when someone criticises you.

   - Migraines.

   - Fear of being late or early.

149

- Fear of driving.

- Dissociation (detaching from your body and your mind wandering elsewhere).

- Eating disorders.

- Need to be liked/people pleasing.

- Need to be better than everyone in the room.

- Hatred of men/women.

- Hating yourself.

- Anxiety or depression or stress.

- Drug/alcohol use.

- Shopping addiction.

- Hoarding money.

- Plastic surgery.

- Excessive working hours.

- Excessive exercising.

There are too many reactions to name but start becoming aware of yours.

> **c. Triggers**: These are things that remind you of the original trauma and 'activate' the traumatic reaction.

Example:

You were attacked by a dog when you were young (trauma). When the attack happened, you became very anxious (traumatic reaction). Now, when a dog walks up to you (trigger), you instantly become anxious.

(Side note: When you are triggered, you regress to who you were when the original trauma happened. A good question to ask yourself when you're triggered, or when someone else is triggered, is: *How old is this person that's triggered right now?*)

3. **Big T and Other T traumas:** Dr Woodhouse teaches that trauma isn't just the obvious 'big' trauma that most people think of when they hear the word. It can also be things such as not having your basic needs met, as mentioned above. She categorises these as 'Big T' and 'Other T' traumas. Here's a list of examples for each (though there are many more):

   a. **Big T Trauma:**

      i.   Rape.

      ii.   War.

      iii. Severe childhood abuse.

      iv.   Witnessing death.

      v.   Severe neglect or abandonment.

      vi.   Catastrophic injuries.

   b. **Other T Trauma:**

      i.   Not having your needs met (being loved, being seen, being heard, being held).

      ii.   Social isolation/rejection.

      iii. Feeling unsafe in your upbringing.

      iv.   Bullying.

      v.   Betrayal.

      vi.   Infidelity.

      vii. Alcoholism or addiction in the home.

      viii. Mental health issues in the home.

Why Am I Sharing All This Information?

When you become aware that you're triggered, you have the ability to try to find the trauma that the trigger is revealing for you. Then, once you've found the original trauma (sometimes you can't because it's in a different body), you can use a tool to heal through that trauma. Then you won't be triggered from that particular trauma/wound anymore (or you will be less triggered).

> *"You will attract people and circumstances*
> *to reveal where you have not healed."*
>
> *– Lewis Huckstep*

Then when your next trigger shows up for you, the process of healing begins again. The graph below shows the flow of healing. Remember that every time you heal, you become less triggered as a whole and you become more authentically expressed.

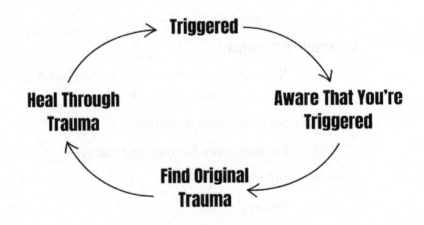

Figure 28

Trauma, Traumatic Reactions and Triggers Summary:

1. Trauma (wound) is what happened or didn't happen to you.

2. Traumatic reaction is the coping strategy that you used to get through the trauma.
3. Triggers are what activate the traumatic reaction and also reveals the trauma.
4. Nothing triggers you; it reveals what's inside of you.

We are now so close to going through the tools to do Inner Work! You need to know just one more thing before doing them, so let's rip straight into it.

Regulating Your Emotions

*"You don't see things the way THEY are,
you see things the way YOU are."*

– Anaïs Nin

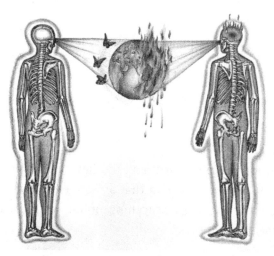

Figure 29[24]

---

[24] David Keil, "We Don't See Things as They Are, We See Things as We Are: Anaïs Nin," *Yoga Anatomy*, accessed September 2, 2024, https://yoga-anatomy.com/we-dont-see-things-as-they-are-we-see-things-as-we-are-anais-nin/.

Within 15 minutes I was in tears, having a full-blown panic attack ...

I wrap up yet another 16-hour day of hustling and grinding, except now the world is in lockdown due to the COVID pandemic, and I have the benefit of not having to drive to and from work, which is kind of nice. Instead, in the morning and afternoon we are running live online home workouts for our clients, and I actually enjoy them.

We were about three months into the lockdowns. So much of the world was filled with fear and uncertainty; however, I wasn't freaking out too much about the whole pandemic/shutdown situation. Maybe I was naïve or maybe I was just avoiding the reality of the situation, but with the JobKeeper scheme (our government paid for employees) along with negotiating free rent with our landlords and our clients being so loyal and supportive – 80% kept paying their normal membership fees to help us – we were actually making more profit during that time.

Something that I had not done for much of my life was watch the mainstream news. The reasons were:

1. I had other things I'd rather do.

2. I learned about world updates through other sources.

3. Mainstream media often uses fearmongering and scare tactics to get viewers to consume their content, because negativity gets more views than positivity does.

I was keeping up to date with all the laws and legislation updates regarding the virus and anything that affected my businesses through friends, family and manually searching online, so most of the time, I didn't consume the TV news.

However, one day I had this random urge to tune into mainstream media to see what was going on in the country and around the world. Within minutes of turning it on, I saw:

- millions of people dying,

- businesses going under,

- restrictions tightening,

- lockdowns extending,

- suicide rates increasing,

- riots building.

Within 15 minutes of watching, I was having a full-blown meltdown, believing things like:

I'm going to lose my businesses.

I'm going to go bankrupt.

My partner will leave me.

I'm a failure.

I can't do this.

... and so many other negative, destructive thoughts.

I went from being positive and optimistic about getting through the pandemic in a healthy way to having a panic attack and crying, thinking about all the horrible things that could happen.

As the quote above says, ***"You don't see things the way THEY are, you see things the way YOU are."***

When you're stressed, you see stress. When you're fearful, you see fear. When you're loving, you see love. When you're abundant, you see abundance.

Because I went from a positive emotional state of mind to a negative emotional state of mind, everything in my world changed. But I knew this information at that time on my journey, so I had the tools to get through. I just needed to come back to neutral. I needed to regulate my emotions.

I took 20 minutes to do some deep circular breathing (you'll learn this soon). I calmed my nervous system, and I got my heartbeat to slow back down. Once I had regulated myself back to neutral, I could then see the world through a balanced lens, not through the fear-driven lens. With my mind and emotions in check, I was able to plan my strategy objectively to navigate the uncertain times of the pandemic ahead.

I was ultimately able to navigate successfully through the pandemic, both with my businesses and home life, with the plan that I created that night. Thankfully, I had been able to calm myself enough to think clearly.

Why Is It Important to Regulate Your Emotions?

When you're drunk or on drugs, you don't see things clearly and you don't make great decisions. So, when you're drunk on emotions, you don't make great decisions either. Your emotions become the filters through which you see the world.

Again, *"You don't see things the way THEY are, you see things the way YOU are."*

Think about the last time you had a big argument. During that argument, when you were in a very negative state of mind, were you thinking of all the positive things about the person you argued with? Absolutely not, because you can't be highly negative and think positively at the same time.

The important point is that whenever you do Inner Work/healing, you must make sure your emotions are as regulated as possible.

Side note - Some healing modalities require you to be in a highly elevated emotional state, such as a rage release exercises.

Think about someone having a panic attack. Do you think that when they are at the peak of that attack it is the right time to start unpacking and healing their traumas? Absolutely not.

The best visual for this is a pendulum. Look at figures 30, 31 and 32 on the next page.

156

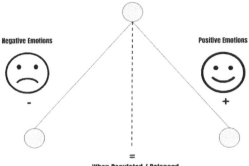

Figure 30

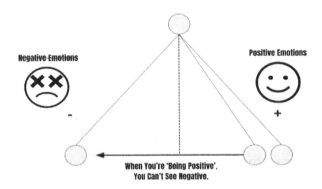

Figure 31

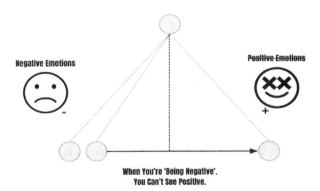

Figure 32

When you're stressed and cortisol enters your bloodstream, you lose up to 50% of your IQ.[25] You're literally thinking and making decisions with half of your brain power.

The next question becomes, how do you regulate your emotions? There are many answers to doing that: meditation, grounding, exercise, breathwork and many more. The one that we're going to use very soon to help with our Inner Work is breathwork.

Breathwork has many different applications depending on what type of breathing you do. The main benefit that we're using it for here is to go from a heightened (positively or negatively) emotional state to a neutral, balanced one. You may have heard or used the terms sympathetic and parasympathetic nervous systems before, or maybe you've heard of polyvagal theory.[26] That's essentially what we're going to do here.

Time to Regulate Your Emotions

This style of breathing is called box breathing, in which we use a five-in, five-hold, five-out count. It's really simple and you can do it whenever you need to regulate your emotions or your nervous system. When you do your breathing, focus on expanding the deep parts of your stomach when you breathe in. This helps a lot with the process.

Let's begin.

The process:

1. Become conscious and place your awareness on your breath.

2. Place one hand on your heart and one hand on your stomach.

---

[25] Kerwin Rae, "Post Content Description," Facebook, August 30, 2024, https://www.facebook.com/kerwinrae/posts/2419964588050604/?paipv= 0&eav=AfYJb9U_qWaiouGqKAiHoMG3QIVA3GZJbhnwTbDQcripk05JKSvluOm 1cj-ktFUzTJk&_rdr.

[26] "Sympathetic Nervous System," *Wikipedia*, last modified August 30, 2024, https://en.wikipedia.org/wiki/Sympathetic_nervous_system.

3. Breathe in through your nose for five seconds (focusing on expanding your stomach and have the intention of breathing in positive energy).

4. Hold it at the top of your breath for five seconds (focusing on expanding your stomach, calming your emotions and nervous system).

5. Breathe out for five seconds through your mouth (focus on letting out any negative emotions or tension).

6. As you breathe, feel the strength of your heart.

7. Repeat this for 2–5 minutes.

I want you to stop reading this book, set a timer for five minutes and practise this breathing technique. For a bonus, play some healing frequencies (search healing frequencies on YouTube or Spotify) and if you can, stand on grass for extra grounding.

How do you feel after that? Take note of the difference within your mental and emotional state and your nervous system. This is the tool we are going to use when:

1. You're feeling overwhelmed/anxious/stressed (or triggered in general).

2. You're doing Inner Work and the emotions become too much, and you need to come back to your breath.

Regulating Emotions Summary:

1. You don't see things the way they are, you see things the way you are.

2. When you're drunk on emotions, you don't see the full picture.

3. Use your breathwork – 5, 5, 5 – when you become aware that you're not neutral with your emotions.

The time has come. You are ready to do the Inner Work. In the following chapters you will be working with three tools to heal. I will be introducing the tool to you at the start of the chapter and then breaking down how the tool works. Then you will be guided through the exercise to heal.

IMPORTANT NOTE:

1. Please do not use these tools if you don't feel like you're ready to do the work.

2. Use your breath to regulate your emotions if they become too much for you.

3. If you reach a breaking point, stop and come back to the exercise when you feel safe and ready to continue.

CHAPTER 10

Dissolving the Ego
- Remove Limiting Beliefs

*"We are born limitless, but we are
programmed out of it."*

– Lewis Huckstep

To make this experience as efficient as possible, I will:

1. Teach you what the Ego is and what Dissolving the Ego means.

2. Show you what the process (tool) is and why we do each step.

3. Share a real-life example of me taking someone through this process.

4. Guide you through the process to heal a wound.

(Side note: The specific wound we are healing in this tool is a limiting belief along with some suppressed emotions. This would fall into the Mental Body and the Emotional Body that we spoke about in previous chapters.)

What Is an Ego?

There are many definitions and views on what an Ego is. Sigmund Freud's teachings on the Ego, Super Ego and Id help a lot with this.[27] To keep things simple, this is my definition:

---

[27] "Sigmund Freud," *Wikipedia*, last modified August 30, 2024, https://en.wikipedia.org/wiki/Sigmund_Freud.

The Ego is the identity of how you view yourself to be and who you believe you need to be to be enough/loved.

Your Ego is the accumulation of all your beliefs, experiences and perceptions (positive and negative). This also includes your wounds and your limiting beliefs. **Your wounds and limiting beliefs only exist in your head.** Think about that for a moment.

There are two traits of the Ego:

1. **It will always prove itself right.**

   Your Ego will make itself right even if it's limiting. If you believe you're not enough, you will make that true by self-sabotaging your goals or by not doing anything towards achieving your goals or by comparing yourself to others. If you fight for your limitations, you get to keep them.

   Example:

   Let's pretend that during your upbringing, you downloaded the belief that you are not worthy of love. Then you get yourself into a relationship. You manage to ruin the relationship through overthinking, feeling unloved, feeling insecure, finding things that aren't even there, and all to prove to yourself that you're not lovable. This is also what people call self-sabotage.

   Picture this:

   - You're born limitless without any limiting beliefs.

   - Then, in your upbringing, you download beliefs that you're not enough.

   - You will always find evidence to reaffirm to yourself that you're not enough , because the Ego always makes itself right.

   - You then either become someone who doesn't achieve anything, or you overcompensate and become an overachiever trying to prove to yourself and the world that you are enough. But you still feel like you're not enough.

This is the wall so many people hit, because their Ego plays the invisible puppet master who is subconsciously controlling their thoughts, decisions, actions and, therefore, results.

2. **It will always avoid pain**.

Your Ego's intention is actually positive. It wants to survive. Our fight-or-flight survival instincts naturally want us to avoid pain; however, the downside is that the Ego will avoid your wounds *because* they are painful. This also means it avoids the opportunity to heal through the wounds. See the problem with this?

The signs the Ego can show up are:

- Justification.

- Deflection.

- Distortion.

- Blame.

- Comparison.

- Attack.

- Overcompensation.

The Ego can show up in many ways, but those above are some of the most common ones.

Example:

You have wounds/insecurities about your weight, and you believe you are fat. Then someone starts questioning you about your weight. Here are some Ego responses:

Justification: Well, I'm overweight because I want to be this shape and it's my own personal choice.

Deflection: Thanks for bringing that up. What are you doing this weekend?

Distortion (sugar-coating): I agree my weight is a problem, but it's not that bad.

Blame: I am overweight but it's because of my parents and my genetics. I'm big-boned.

Defence: Why do you care about my weight? It's none of your business.

Comparison: I agree I am a little overweight, but have you seen John? He's way worse than me.

Denial: I don't know what you're talking about. I'm not overweight.

Attack: Fuck you. You're just saying this because of ...

Overcompensation: I don't need to lose weight. Have you seen how much money I make and how beautiful my car is?

Which one is your Ego's favourite flavour? Mine is overcompensation and deflection.

(Side note: Become aware of when these traits of the Ego show up. When they do, the Ego is either trying to avoid a wound or it's fighting to make itself right.)

Reminder: All your beliefs, positive and negative, are a part of your Ego. Think of when you buy a new phone or computer. It comes with its default settings and programming to allow it to work properly. This is positive programming (positive beliefs). However, if your phone or computer downloads a virus, it's not going to run efficiently, and it will start shutting down and malfunctioning. This is the negative programming (negative beliefs). The goal is to identify and dissolve the negative beliefs (the virus).

For ease of communication, when I use the term Ego, I am referring to the limiting (negative) beliefs of your Ego. When I use the term True Authentic Self, I am referring to the limitless (positive) beliefs of your Ego.

Your Ego (negative beliefs) I picture as the bandages on a mummy, where each bandage represents a limiting belief. Each limiting belief/bandage hides or limits your True Authentic Self, who is underneath it all.

Figure 33

Figure 34 is how I picture a True Authentic Self –- a baby with all the limitless potential and possibility, and none of the negative programming.

Figure 34[28]

Michelangelo's famous quote about David aligns with this really well.

Figure 35[29]

Someone asked how he made the beautiful statue of David, Michelangelo said, *"Easy, David was always in the statue, I just chipped away anything that wasn't him."*[30]

Remember my definition of Inner Work:

"To dissolve/heal the wounds and blockages that are masking your true self."

---

[28] Ira Israel, "No Child Was Ever Born with Low Self-Esteem," *Ira Israel,* accessed September 2, 2024, https://iraisrael.com/no-child-was-ever-born-with-low-self-esteem/.

[29] Euronews, "Culture Re-View: Unveiloed Today in 1504, Here are 5 Intriguing Facts About Michaelangelo's David," *Euronews,* last modified September 8, 2023, https://www.euronews.com/culture/2023/09/08/culture-re-view-unveiled-today-in-1504-here-are-5-intriguing-facts-about-michelangelos-dav.

[30] Euronews, "5 Intriguing Facts About Michaelangelo's David."

It's about identifying the parts that are limiting you (negative beliefs of the Ego) and healing/dissolving through it. This reveals the limitless version of you that is underneath (your True Authentic Self).

Let's break down the quote: *"We are born limitless, but we are programmed out of it."*

What does that mean? Have you ever met a baby/child, who's first words are, *'I'm not enough'*? No, I haven't either. Why? Because we are born as infinite, limitless, spiritual beings. We are our **True Authentic Self**, perfect and enough by just BEING who we are. We don't need money or status or cars or houses, a great body or anything external to feel that we are enough.

However, from the moment you were born, you have picked up/downloaded beliefs of who you are and who you need to be to be enough in the world (your Ego). Here are some common examples:

- I'm not enough.
- I must be on time.
- I have to have money to be successful.
- Showing emotions is weak.
- I need to look after everyone else.
- I'm broken.
- I'm not smart enough.
- It's my fault.
- I'm too much.
- My needs don't matter.
- I'm a failure.
- Life is scary.
- Money is evil.
- I'm ugly.

- I can't trust anyone.
- Love is painful.
- I'm not worthy of love.
- I can't do anything right.
- I'm too old.
- I'm too young.
- I have to be perfect.

Notice how simple and short these are. When you do the Ego Dissolving Process, you want to get the belief into its most basic form.

There's an infinite amount of limiting beliefs. Start to become aware of what yours are because we're about to get rid of one of them very soon. All these limitations cover and suppress your True Authentic Self. Think of the difference like this:

True Authentic Self: Who you are <u>without</u> all the limiting beliefs you've downloaded.

Ego: Who you are <u>with</u> all the limiting beliefs you've downloaded.

Another powerful visual for your True Authentic Self, someone who is fully conscious and present. They are a full expression of who they are. Figure 36. does this for me:

Figure 36

The Aim of the Game

Identify all your subconscious (sometimes conscious) beliefs that are limiting you (your Ego), and then 'dissolve' them. In doing so, you allow your True Authentic Self to shine through. Each time you dissolve a limitation, you access more of your potential and tap into the true essence of who you are.

> *"Your light shines brightest when you let it shine freely."*
> – Lewis Huckstep

How do you identify your limitations? There are four ways:

1. Most people are aware of some of their limiting beliefs (conscious).

2. Be conscious of when you're triggered, find the trauma it's come from and then you will be able to find the limitation there (unconscious).

3. Someone who has enough awareness can reflect back to you a limiting belief of which you weren't aware (unconscious).

4. Use a probing tool from a coach/healer/therapist (unconscious).

Remember these four ways, because you will be using them when you do your process.

Dissolving the Ego Summary:

1. **True Authentic Self**: Who you are, <u>without</u> all the limiting beliefs you've downloaded.

   Ego: Who you are, <u>with</u> all the limiting beliefs you've downloaded.

2. Your Ego will prove itself right, even if it's limiting. It will also avoid pain, which prevents you from healing.

3. The aim of the game is to identify all your subconscious (sometimes conscious) beliefs that are limiting you (your Ego), and then 'dissolve' them.

Healing Is in the Feeling

Imagine that you're walking with a bag on your back and you're in a rush to get somewhere, when someone comes up to you and hurts you mentally, emotionally and physically. They cause negative feelings to come up: shame, fear, guilt, and grief, but because you're in a rush, instead of giving yourself the time and space to process (feel) through these emotions, you just suppress and stuff them into your bag.

This is what the majority of people do for their entire lives. They continue to avoid feeling their emotions and choose to suppress them instead. This results in carrying around a massive weight of emotions on their back, which constantly drains them mentally, emotionally and spiritually, and manifests in their body physically. Everything that has been suppressed can also become a trigger, until you heal (feel) through it.

One massive component to healing is feeling (the Emotional Body). Instead of suppressing and avoiding the emotions, it's about actually facing them head on and 'feeling through them'. Feel it once and for all, so you don't have to keep feeling it. This is why the regulating emotions tool is so important to be able to bring yourself back to neutral if the emotions become too much.

When we go through the process, I will instruct you to feel the emotions as much as you can, to clear the suppressed ones out. This is why the healing is in the feeling.

Figure 37[31]

Universal Truth

To use this particular tool for healing, there is something that you need to understand.

---

[31] Christian International School, "Post Content Description," Facebook, August 30, 2020, https://www.facebook.com/ChristianInternationalSchool /photos/a.614053535334025/3641130189292996/?type=3&source=48&pa ipv=0&eav=Afac6UZWU-FCjYhPHTcKvYlRBWtgcSxaG7KjvSZgFsGUMMB6T3 cadkgVF2lU-BroSZw&_rdr.

A universal truth is something that is 'always true'.[32] It will never not be true. Depending what lens and beliefs you view this through, it can get very foggy as to what is a universal truth and what isn't.

Examples:

- Gravity on earth is a universal truth. It doesn't matter if you're in Australia, America, China or anywhere around the world, gravity is always consistent.

- Your human body will die and decay. For 100% of people in history, the 'meat suit' that we live our life in, will eventually die and decay away. Your soul however may be reborn into the next meat suit (depending on your spiritual/religious beliefs).

- Life is uncertain. Today, tomorrow, next week, next year, 10 years or 50 years from now, we are never sure what's going to happen in life.

Remember, for something to be a universal truth, it must be true 100% of the time. It can never not be true.

Why Is This Important?

This is important, because all of your limiting beliefs (your Ego) are NOT universal truths, you've just downloaded them.

If you've been paying attention, all of your beliefs, both positive and negative are a part of your Ego. So, your limitless empowering beliefs are also NOT universal truths, but just like the phone or computer with their default programming and viruses, we want to keep the good programming (limitless beliefs/True Authentic Self) and remove the viruses (limiting beliefs/Ego).

---

[32] Lanh Ho, "Sartre's Concept of Freedom," *Reflections: A Journal of Philosophical Inquiry,* 2006, California State University, East Bay, https://www.csueastbay.edu/philosophy/reflections/2006/contents/lanh-ho.html.

Once you dissolve a limitation, what you're left with is the True Authentic Self. It's like removing a bandage from the mummy in (Fig. 33) and then revealing your True Authentic Self who was always underneath.

When we do the Ego Dissolving Process in a moment, please remember that a universal truth is always true. There cannot be a single reference of it not being true.

Real-Life Coaching Session Example

I took a client through the Ego Dissolving Process. For this example, I will put side notes (using *) next to the important steps, so you can understand how the process works and get more out of doing the process yourself.

I was on a coaching session with a client we'll call Sally.

Sally was a sales manager for a team of 15 sales reps. I asked Sally, "What can I help you with in today's session?" She responded with, "I get really <u>anxious</u> when I speak in front of my team." "Interesting," I said. "That sounds like it's a trigger from a past wound. Would you like to heal through that now?" "Yes please," she replied.

I took Sally through some breathwork to regulate her emotions and calm her nervous system.

(*Similar to the technique that you learned in the previous chapter.)

We also did a bonus visualisation exercise.

(*I always recommend doing some breathwork before, during and after doing most forms of Inner Work – you'll learn about this when you do the process yourself)

After we finished the breathwork, this is how the coaching session went:

Lewis: "What is it specifically that makes you feel nervous about speaking in front of those people?"

(*Here, I'm looking for the specific trigger.)

Sally: "Being embarrassed."

(*I know that <u>embarrassment</u> is the trigger.)

Lewis: "When was the first memory you have of being embarrassed in front of others?"

(*I'm looking for the original trauma/wound where she downloaded a limitation.)

She takes a while to find it, but when she does, she starts to get emotional straightaway.

Sally: "I was six years old in Year One. The teacher handed out cards for the kids to write on. The cards had two lines on them, and you had to write down how you would describe yourself. I wrote down on the first line: I'm pretty. On the second line: nice to people. We then gave the cards back to the teacher."

By this point Sally was crying.

Sally continues: "The teacher read out my card, but she only read the first line: I'm pretty. The whole class started to laugh. I was really overweight and insecure back then. I started to cry, and I ran out of the room."

(*I believed this was the original trauma/wound.)

Lewis: "What was the feeling you experienced in that moment?"

(*Now I'm identifying which emotion is linked to this experience and is probably suppressed.)

Sally: "I felt so much shame."

Lewis: "I want you to really feel that emotion for me right now."

(*The healing is in the feeling.)

Lewis: "I want you to double the feeling. Really feel it."

Lewis: "I want you to 10x the feeling. Feel it now so you don't have to feel it ever again."

Sally is crying and releasing a lot of emotions at this point.

(*She's healing.)

Lewis: "Well done for having the strength for going there. Come back to your breathing and calm down your nervous system."

(*She's now regulating her emotions and nervous system to be able to do the next step of this process.)

Lewis: "Now, in that moment at the peak of the experience, through the eyes of your six- year-old self, what was the meaning that you created about yourself or about the world?"

(*I'm asking her to look for the limiting belief (Ego).)

Sally: "I'm worthless."

(*This is the limiting belief.)

Lewis: "I want you to give me three references of this belief <u>not</u> being true."

(*I'm proving that this isn't a universal truth – This part can be hard, because the Ego will also prove itself right. But references of the belief not being true can always be found, if you just keep looking.)

Sally: "My partner loving me. My children giving me love. Having a career."

Lewis: "Beautiful. Now, if I were to cut you open like for an operation, would I find a manufacturing stamp inside of you, saying, 'Sally Brown, born in Australia and she is not worthy?'"

Sally: "No."

Lewis: "The reason why is because you weren't born with it."

Sally nods.

Lewis: "Beautiful. So, if a universal truth always has to be consistent and you've given me three references of it not being true, and you weren't born with it, what does that mean about this belief?"

Sally: "It's not true."

Lewis: "Well done. I'm going to ask you three questions and you can only answer yes or no."

Lewis: "Is this belief that you're worthless true? Yes or no?"

(*This part can also be hard, because the Ego will also prove itself right. But the answer is no. If the answer is yes, go back and find more references of this belief not being true).

Sally: "No."

Lewis: "I want you to say this answer with every cell in your body. Is this belief that you're worthless true? Yes or no?"

Sally: "No."

Lewis: "Breathe that into you. One more time, say it with everything you have, and I want you to feel it through your body. Is this belief that you're worthless true? Yes or no?"

Sally: "No."

Lewis: "Now, I want you really to feel, see and experience everything at a 10/10 level when I ask you the next question. How does your whole life and reality change, with this belief not there anymore?"

(*This is about experiencing and seeing life as your True Authentic Self.)

Sally's shoulders drop. Her energy shifts. She has a huge smile.

Sally: "I feel lighter. I feel happy. I feel free. I feel like I am enough."

Lewis: "How does your day-to-day life change with this belief not there?"

176

Sally: "I speak my truth. I show up more as who I truly am. I don't compare myself to others. I'm a better leader for my team. I'm a better mother for my kids. I'm a better partner for my husband."

Lewis: "What emotions become available to you with this belief not there?"

Sally: "Happiness. Joy. Love. Gratitude. Strength. Abundance."

Lewis: "Please really feel them at a 10/10 level."

Sally nods.

Lewis: "With this belief not there anymore, which belief replaces it?"

(*Now I am revealing the True Authentic Self.)

Sally: "I am worthy, and I am enough."

Lewis: "Feel that now for me."

After we have regulated and come back to neutral, I ask Sally when her next meeting with her sales team is due and learn that it is actually on the next day. I ask her, "How are you feeling about the meeting with the sales team now?" She says, "For the first time ever, I actually feel excited and peaceful about it."

Pretty powerful, right?

Finding the Wound/Limiting Belief on Which to Do the Process

You are about to go through the Ego Dissolving Process! First, though, you need to decide which limiting belief or wound you are going to do the process on.

Remember that there are four ways to find which wound to heal through:

1. Most people are aware of some of their own limiting beliefs.

2. Be conscious of when you're triggered, find the trauma and where it's come from. You will be able to find the limitation there. You'll know once you go through the process.

3. Someone who has enough awareness can reflect back to you a limiting belief of which you were not aware.

4. Use a probing tool from a coach/healer/therapist.

Because each option requires different variations of questions to do the process, we will just be using the last one for now. (As I said before, there are too many variations to fit even into this book, but I do provide all of the other variations in my Conscious Community.) In this instance, I will provide you with the probing tool/probing question as you go through the process.

Your Turn: Ego Dissolving

The time has come to do your own Inner Work!

Here's the checklist:

1. Make sure you're in a safe environment with no distractions. Schedule at least 45 minutes to do this properly. Ask your family to leave you alone. Put the phone away.

2. If you're reading this and doing the work on yourself, I'd recommend that you read each question, then close your eyes and really tune into your intuition to answer them.

   a. I've recorded a video of me taking you through this process. Here's the link www.lewishuckstep.com/book or scan this QR code:

178

b. If you wish, you can get someone to read out the questions and take you through this process. This will allow you to focus just on your breath and to answer the questions authentically.

3. You can write down your answers as you go through the process, or you can think, feel and see them in your mind/body.

4. When I ask you to 'feel the emotions', really feel this at the highest level you can. Get to a 10/10 level with the feelings. Remember, the healing is in the feeling.

5. Remember to continue to breathe throughout the entire process to regulate your emotions as best you can.

6. If the emotions become too much for you, just stop, come back to your breath and try again when you feel ready.

7. Remember that this is a very intuitive process. If you start overthinking, come back to your breath and tune into your intuition.

Do this process as many times as you want to. There's always more healing to be done. I'd recommend doing a process (not just this process, but any healing modality/tool) once a week.

Let's begin.

Sit down and get comfortable, and then:

1. Place one hand on your heart and your other hand on your stomach. Start to tune into your breath. In through the nose, deep into your stomach and out through the mouth. In for five seconds, hold for five seconds, out for five seconds. Feeling the strength of your heart with every breath in.

2. Give your heart and intuition the permission to lead the way with this process. **Allow whatever answers that come up for you to be spoken.**

3. What is your first memory of you feeling like you weren't enough?

_____

_____

(Take your time with this. If you get in your head, take a deep breath and ask yourself the question again.)

4. How old were you when this experience happened? Whatever the first number that comes up is the right answer.

_____

    a. Through the eyes of your younger self, what did you experience?

_____

_____

_____

_____

    b. What was the core emotion you felt at this time?

_____

_____

_____

_____

5. I want you to feel that emotion as much as you can. Feel it properly, so you don't have to feel it again.

    a. I want you to double the intensity of the feeling.

    b. I want you to 5x the intensity of the feeling.

    c. I want you to 10x the intensity of the feeling.

6. Well done. Come back to your breath. Focus on regulating your emotions and nervous system.

7. Looking through the eyes of your younger self and using the words you used back then:

   a. What was the meaning that you decided about yourself or about the world?

   _____

   _____

(Take your time to get this. Remember to look through the eyes of your younger self and word it as you did back then. Keep it short, simple and direct.)

   b. Now, remember this limiting belief for the following questions.

8. Now, I want you to find three references of this belief <u>not</u> being true.

   _____

   _____

   _____

   a. Look through your Values.

   b. Look through family, friends, relationships, career, business and anything else.

   c. Keep looking until you find at least three references, if not more.

   d. I guarantee that you can find them. Do not move on until you find at least three.

9. Now, if I were to cut you open, would I find a manufacturer's stamp saying: Your name, born in whatever country you're born in, stating that you have this limiting belief?

_____

    a.   The answer is no.

    b.   If you said yes, your Ego is fighting to keep this limitation. Take a deep breath, go find more references of this not being true and ask yourself this question again.

10. Why won't I find this manufacturer's stamp inside you?

_____

_____

    a.   The answer is: You weren't born with it.

11. Remember what a universal truth is? It must always be true. It can never not be true. If you weren't born with this belief and you have given at least three references to show that this belief isn't consistent, what does it mean about this belief?

_____

_____

    a.   The answer is: It's not the truth.

12. The next three questions I'm going to ask you can only be answered with a yes or no.

13. Is this belief true? Yes or no?

_____

    a.   The answer is no.

14. Say this with every cell in your body. Is this belief true? Yes or no?

a. The answer is no.

15. Breathe that in. One more time and I want you to feel this in every cell in your body. Is this belief true? Yes or no?

The answer is no.

16. Now when I ask you the next question, I want you to feel, see and experience everything at a 10/10 level. How does your whole life and reality change, with this belief not there?

a. Spend your time experiencing, seeing and feeling this answer.

b. What else changes?

c. Notice your lungs, your shoulders, your nervous system.

17. How does your day-to-day life change with this belief not there?

_____

_____

18. What feelings become available to you with this belief not there?

_____

_____

    a. Feel these feelings as much as you can.

19. With this belief not there anyone, what replaces that belief?

_____

_____

    a. How does that feel to you?

_____

_____

    b. Feel this at a 10/10 level.

20. Come back to your normal breathing. Notice the difference in your nervous system, your body and your heart.

21. Once I count down from three, bring your awareness back into your body. I then want you to write down everything that you experienced during this process.

22. "Three, two, one."

Write down everything that you experienced in this process:

_____

_____

_____

_____

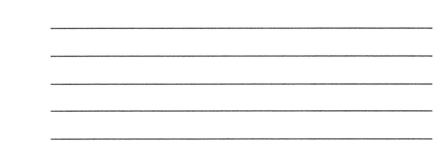

Congratulations!!! How do you feel right now? What do you notice differently? Do you feel lighter? Do you feel more present? Do you feel more love? Do you feel less resistant?

If you'd like to send me a message on any of my social media accounts (Instagram is best at the time of writing) and share your experience of doing this exercise, I'd be forever grateful for that. If you'd like to leave a review on Amazon as well, that would mean so much to me – and it would only take a minute of your time. Just head to your Amazon account, go to my book's listing and leave a review.

What you just experienced is my own unique healing tool that I've created using three modalities and 10 years of experience. Here are some tips for the integration part:

- Take some time for yourself in the next week to just sit with yourself, to allow yourself to connect with how you're feeling and how you're processing everything.

- Become aware of your new empowering belief that replaced (was underneath) the old limiting belief. Every reference you find to affirm this new belief makes it stronger.

Now I want to give you another really powerful resource that will help you to continue to do more and more Inner Work. This resource will help you with the '*Ego Dissolving Process*' you just went through and with the '*Balancing Process*' we're about to do.

It is called the **Trigger Hit List**.

Remember that nothing triggers you, it just reveals what's inside you, an unhealed trauma/wound.

Well, what if you could document every time you get triggered, so that when you have the time and space to heal, you have a whole list of triggers to heal through? That's exactly what this resource is.

Side note – when you are triggered, it is either a limiting belief or a trauma being revealed. The more you become conscious of your triggers, the better you'll become in determining if it is a limiting belief or a trauma.

(Turn to page 239 to find the Trigger Hit List.)

This is how you use this tool for doing the Inner Work:

1. Become aware that you're triggered or that you're judging something within someone (you don't like someone for some reason).

2. Determine if it is a limiting belief or trauma being revealed. Then ask yourself:

   a. What is the specific trait that triggered me, or that I'm judging this person for? It must be a one-word answer.

   b. What limiting belief is being triggered?

3. Write the person's name or the event, the date and the trait or the limiting belief into the table.

4. Write down which process you will use:

   a. If it is a trait, do the Balancing Process

   b. If it is a limiting belief, do the Ego Dissolving Process

5. Set aside time to do your own healing work.

The reality is that when you get triggered at work– when you're with friends or family or anything else – you probably won't be able to go through and heal it there and then, but you can use the regulating emotions tool to help you in the moment (5, 5, 5 breathing). However, by writing down all of these triggers and becoming aware of the limiting belief or trauma that's being triggered, you will gain the awareness to be able to do your Inner Work when you have the time and space to do so.

You also can easily just write these into notes on your phone.

Status update ...

Figure 38

Well done!!! We're so close to finishing our journey together through *The Inspired Life Method*. Now that you've gone through the *Ego Dissolving Process*, you're going to go through two more processes. When I really started doing my inner work, this next process had the most amount of impact on me with my healing journey. It is insanely powerful, and I know it'll change your life forever. Let's do it.

CHAPTER 11

Balancing Perceptions - Heal Trauma

"Any emotion that you experience outside
of love and gratitude is a lopsided perception."
– Dr John Demartini [33]

Remember the story I shared of my dad breaking down my brother's door to hurt him? I actually healed that specific trauma using this tool that you're about to experience.

This process is modelled after the *'Demartini Method'* created by Dr John Demartini. John's method is the most powerful process I have experienced when it comes to healing the 'Mental Body'. His method will heal any mental trauma, judgements, memories or anything of which you are aware.

I have trained with Dr Demartini, and I am a Demartini Facilitator. I will be taking you through an altered version of his method so we can integrate the Emotional Body more into this healing process.

Disclaimer: I am not the creator of the Demartini Method. Full credits to The Demartini Institute.

This method is so powerful that it takes a fair bit of teaching to understand the process and fully 'get it'. I recommend reading the book *The Breakthrough Experience* by Dr John Demartini and even attending his event of the same name if you can. However, I will do my best to teach this method as simply as possible.

---

[33] Demartini, "What Is the Purpose of Life?"

Perceptions

Firstly, what is a perception? The Google definition: *The way in which something is regarded, understood or interpreted.*

Think about perceptions like this:

When you watch a movie/video, you're not watching a video, you're watching thousands if not millions of photos stacked back-to-back to back. When we get up to doing the 'Balancing Process', you want to focus on the 'single photo' of the situation, because our perceptions are created in moments (single images). Remember this for later.

Every single one of the 7.9 billion people on this planet will have different perceptions of different situations, depending on their beliefs, conditioning and biases.

This quote puts it really nicely:

"Everything we hear is an opinion, not a fact. Everything we see is a perspective, not the truth." – Marcus Aurelius[34]

Figure 39 is a great representation of this concept. If you remember back to the chapter on the Ego, the Ego will always prove itself right. So, if you have a perception that *'something you experienced was so traumatic that you can never heal from it and that you're broken forever'*, then that's what your Ego will make true.

---

[34] George Marcus, "Everything We Hear Is an Opinion, Not a Fact. Everything We See Is a Perspective, Not the Truth," *Philosiblog*, December 14, 2015, https://philosiblog.com/2015/12/14/everything-we-hear-is-an-opinion-not-a-fact-everything-we-see-is-a-perspective-not-the-truth/.

Figure 39[35]

Let's view this through a physics lens.

Physics states that there is total balance. In simple terms the law is that for every action there is an equal and opposite reaction. Everything exists with its equal and opposite. In physics, it's called Newton's third law. In spirituality it's yin and yang. In the practical world it's hot and cold. In the universe it's matter and anti-matter.[36]

This simply means that life is always balanced, that you can't have a positive without a negative and you can't have a negative without a positive. However, our own perceptions are very often lopsided.

The goal of the *Balancing Process* is to bring every lopsided perception into balance.

Let's use some examples:

---

[35] Veldhoen + Company, "A Different Perspective," *Veldhoen + Company Blog,* accessed September 2, 2024, https://www.veldhoencompany.com/blog/a-different-perspective.

[36] Shawn Cook, "The Theory of Everything Resolved," *Medium,* last modified July 19, 2022, https://medium.com/@shawn.cook/the-theory-of-everything-resolved-76d25e962241.

Someone goes through a relationship in which they are cheated on and abused both mentally and emotionally.

Person 1 (negative perception):

- I've just wasted so much of my time.

- I've been so hurt; I won't be able to trust anyone again.

- I'll be single forever.

- I'm broken and I won't be able to heal from this.

- This is the worst thing that's ever happened to me.

Person 2 (positive perception):

- I've invested time to learn what I don't want in a relationship.

- I've been gifted awareness about who to trust and what signs to look out for.

- I'm grateful that we ended the relationship now, so I have time to attract the right partner into my life.

- I get to heal from this hurt and turn this pain into Purpose /strength.

- This is the best thing that ever happened for me.

See the difference? It's the perception that each person has on each situation.

An example of someone of whom you might have heard:

Oprah Winfrey was sexually abused six times, by family members and family friends.[37] Her family also physically abused her: "[My grandmother] whipped me so badly that I had welts on my back and the

---

[37] Joelle Goldstein, "Oprah Winfrey Details Own Abuse Months Before Interviewing Michael Jackson Accusers," *People*, February 27, 2019, https://people.com/tv/oprah-winfrey-details-own-abuse-months-before-interviewing-michael-jackson-accusers/.

welts would bleed," Oprah said in an interview.[38] She lived in boarding houses in poverty-stricken cities, she experienced racism throughout her life, she had a baby – which died shortly after birth – when she was 14.[39] [40]

Despite all the challenges she experienced in her upbringing, she achieved more than most people ever will. Here are just some of her accomplishments:

- Producer, actress and television icon.

- First black American woman to own a production company.

- Academy Award nominee.

- Was once television's highest-paid entertainer.

- Host of a television talk show that reached 15 million people a day.

- Author.

- Donated $400 million to higher education, including 400 scholarships.

- Presidential Medal of Freedom.

---

[38] Learning Liftoff, "Overcoming Obstacles: What Oprah Winfrey Learned from Her Abusive Childhood," *Learning Liftoff*, accessed September 2, 2024, https://learningliftoff.com/college/college-scholarships/overcoming-obstacles-what-oprah-winfrey-learned-from-her-abusive-childhood/.

[39] Elephant Learning, "Oprah Winfrey: From Poverty to World-Famous Broadcaster & Philanthropist," *Elephant Learning*, accessed September 2, 2024, https://www.elephantlearning.com/post/oprah-winfrey-from-poverty-to-world-famous-broadcaster-philanthropist#:~:text=Sadly%2C%20young%20Winfrey%20suffered%20years,out%20of%20the%20house%20working.&text=It%20was%20a%20traumatic%20time,Winfrey%2C%20in%20Nashville%2C%20Tennessee.

[40] Larry King, "Oprah Winfrey Opens Up About Her Abusive Childhood (2007)," YouTube video, 4:52, posted by Larry King, August 15, 2020, https://www.youtube.com/watch?v=fh4524Lp0aM

- Honorary doctorates from Duke University and Harvard University.

- 18 Daytime Emmy Awards.

- Net worth $US2.8 billion at end of 2023.

Impressive to say the least. So how can people who go through similar traumatic experiences as (and much less than) Oprah, but end up using their trauma as excuses instead of fuel? Listen to how Oprah speaks about her life and how her experiences shaped her.

"It was because I was sexually abused and raped that I have such empathy for people who have experienced that. It was because I was raised poor, had no running water and was getting whippings, that I have such compassion for people who have experienced it. It has given me a broader understanding and a deeper appreciation for every little and big thing that I now have. I am so grateful for my years literally living in poverty. My story just helped define and shape me, as does everybody's story."

In short, Oprah's perception of her life is one that served her, not one that limited her.

Here's one more real-life example to drive this home:

Viktor Frankl spent two-and-a-half years as a concentration camp prisoner in World War II. He experienced physical abuse, malnutrition, emotional humiliation and torture. His wife and parents were also prisoners in the camps and were killed.

(Due to the graphic nature of what was experienced during this period, I won't be writing about the specifics of all things that Viktor endured. However, please do yourself a favour and read his book, *Man's Search for Meaning*.)

The reason I share this with you is that Viktor experienced one of the most horrific events in history, survived it and came out the other side with a positive outlook on life. Here are some quotes from him:

"I can see beyond the misery of the situation to the potential for discovering a meaning behind it, and thus to turn an apparently meaningless suffering into a genuine human achievement. I am convinced that, in the final analysis, there is no situation that does not contain within it the seed of meaning."

"Everything can be taken from a man but one thing: the last of human freedoms – to choose one's attitude in any given set of circumstances, to choose one's own way."

"Between stimulus and response, there is a space. In that space is our power to choose our response. In our response lies our growth and our freedom."

Again, how can someone experience so much hurt, suffering and pain, and yet have a positive outlook and attitude towards life? It was his perception of the circumstances.

**"There is nothing either good or bad,
but thinking makes it so."**

- Hamlet

Emotional vs Transcendent Feelings

Dr Demartini teaches the difference between emotional feelings and transcendent feelings. This teaching really aligns well with Dr David Hawking's Scale of Consciousness (shown in figure 40.) As you can see, the more 'negative' emotions are at the bottom of the scale, while the 'positive' emotions are towards the top:

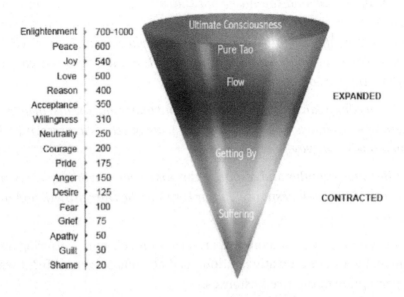

Enlightenment	700-1000
Peace	600
Joy	540
Love	500
Reason	400
Acceptance	350
Willingness	310
Neutrality	250
Courage	200
Pride	175
Anger	150
Desire	125
Fear	100
Grief	75
Apathy	50
Guilt	30
Shame	20

Figure 40[41]

Let's define an emotional feeling vs a transcendent feeling.

An **'emotional feeling'** is what Demartini would call a lopsided or unbalanced perception. This means that you are perceiving more positives than negatives, or more negatives than positives in a situation, which would be anything below Love (500) on the scale of consciousness (Fig. 40)

A **'transcendent feeling'** is what he calls a synthesised/integrated /balanced perception. This means that you are perceiving an equal number of positives and negatives to a situation, which would be Love (500 and above) on the scale of consciousness. (Fig. 40)

---

41 Saumya Dave, "What David Hawkins Taught Us About the Emotional Scale of Consciousness and Achieving Higher Levels," *Medium*, Readers Digests (blog), January 29, 2020, https://medium.com/readers-digests/what-david-hawkins-taught-us-about-the-emotional-scale-of-consciousness-and-achieving-higher-levels-a21b337b534d.

Remember the quote at the start of this chapter? "**Any emotion that you experience outside of love and gratitude is a lopsided perception.**" This means that if you can't genuinely feel love and gratitude to anything or anyone in life, you have a lopsided/unbalanced perception.

Let's use some pendulums again:

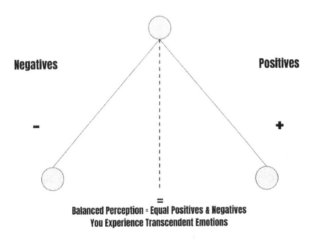

Figure 41

A balanced perception (Fig. 41) is seeing equal amounts of positives and negatives to a situation/person. As a result, you will experience transcendent emotions/feelings such as love, gratitude, joy and peace. This can be called 'putting someone in your heart'.

Think of the positive person in the earlier relationship example who was grateful for the relationship ending.

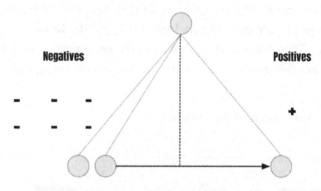

Lopsided Perception = More Negatives Than Positives
You Experience Negative Emotions: Shame, Guilt, Fear, Anger, etc.

Figure 42

A negative lopsided perception (Fig. 42) is where you perceive more negatives than positives in a situation/person. As a result, you will experience negative emotions/feelings such as shame, guilt, fear, anger, frustration, sadness, etc. This can also be called 'putting someone in the pit'.

Think of the negative person in the earlier relationship example who was angry and hurt from the break-up.

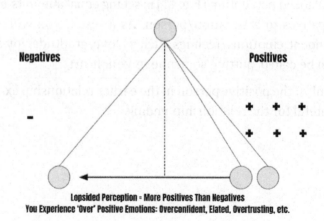

Lopsided Perception = More Positives Than Negatives
You Experience 'Over' Positive Emotions: Overconfident, Elated, Overtrusting, etc.

Figure 43

A positive lopsided perception (Fig. 43) is where you perceive more positives than negatives to a situation/person. As a result, you will experience unbalanced positive emotions/feelings such as overconfidence, pride, over-trusting, over-caring, etc. This can be called 'putting someone on a pedestal'.

Think of the early stages of a relationship (honeymoon period), when everything is sunshine, rainbows, hot steamy sex and no fights. Then, because life (the universe) will always find balance, once the honeymoon period finishes, you start noticing all the skeletons in your partner's closet, all the things that irritate you, and you start triggering each other. You start balancing your perception of your partner.

Here's a life-changing tip: Life (the universe) will always find balance. You can balance yourself out (using the Balancing Process) or the universe will do it for you. However, the universe can sometimes do it in very painful ways.

Think of hindsight:

You go through something 'bad'. A day, a week, a month, a year, a decade or multiple decades pass, then something clicks, and you realise the 'bad' thing that you went through actually served you. How do you turn that hindsight from years into seconds? That's what the Balancing Process does.

How Does This Help with Healing?

Do you remember when we discussed trauma, traumatic reactions and triggers?

"Trauma is unprocessed memories." I prefer to say, "unprocessed experiences".

A question to ask is: How do you process memories/experiences?

Answer: Use the Demartini Method or my altered version: the Balancing Process.

You could also redefine trauma as: **"...a lopsided perception."** (Trauma in the Mental Body)

This means that if you have any trauma or judgement (lopsided perception) towards any person or any situation, you can use the Demartini Method or the Balancing Process to heal (balance) that trauma. Read this paragraph again – it's pretty powerful.

You're very close to going through this process yourself. There are just a few more things to understand about it...

More Context for Balancing

This method can be hard to understand fully if you've been through any 'Big T' traumas of the kind mentioned earlier in this chapter.

"What are the benefits of being abused/raped/abandoned/ neglected, etc?"

As difficult as it might be to understand right now, everything can be balanced/healed. I have done this process with clients who have, among other traumatic experiences:

- been sexually assaulted/raped

- been abandoned by parents

- had broken up with a partner, 36 hours later walked into their house to find this person (the ex) had decapitated his own head

- had business partners take advantage of them and take all their money

- had a partner who committed suicide

- had a mother tell them at six years old 'I wish I had an abortion instead of having you'

- attempted suicide themselves

Dr Demartini has countless examples of people who have gone through the most horrific events yet who, by the end of this process, were in tears of gratitude.

Here are two examples that Dr Demartini shared when I attended his *Breakthrough Experience* program:

There was a woman who attended his in-person event. Everyone was taking the lunch break, and she was talking on the phone to her husband. Her phone was on loudspeaker, and everyone present heard her husband shoot himself dead. The woman burst into tears. Dr Demartini brought her to the front with him and took her through his Demartini Process. Within hours, the entire trauma/wound/perception was healed/balanced. Yes, that can be hard to believe until you experience the process yourself.

Dr Demartini was asked to do a presentation at a jail to help inmates with their own growth journey. Many of the inmates were in jail for murder. Among them was a man who had murdered a married man whose wife was also at the presentation. These people obviously didn't like each other. Dr Demartini took that woman and that man (her husband's killer) through his Demartini Method. Within three hours, the man and woman were hugging each other in tears of gratitude. Again, this can be hard to understand until you go through the process yourself.

We All Express All Traits

Demartini went on a mission to help him understand more about human behaviour and why we judge others for things that we do ourselves. He grabbed the Oxford English Dictionary and went through it line by line to find every human trait that someone can express. The end result was 4628 traits. Each time he found a trait, he looked through his life until he found a time when he had expressed it. This happened for all 4628 traits. Why? Because every human expresses all traits.

I'm a nice person. I'm also a mean person. I've lied before. I've been honest before. I've been loving to someone. I've been cruel to someone. I've displayed the trait of addiction before. I've been positive. I've been negative.

When you judge someone for having a 'negative' trait, you disown and block out that trait in yourself, even though you've shown the same trait in your life, in another form. Now, a key part of that sentence is 'in another form'. You might not have said hurtful words out loud to someone in the exact form that you're judging someone for, but you will have said other hurtful words to someone or even yourself inside your own head. So, remember to look into the other forms where you've displayed the trait, look in the seven areas of life—spiritual, mental, vocational, financial, familial, social, and physical.

Dr Demartini has taken well over 100,000 clients through his process, and every person (the ones willing to look properly) has found and owned the fact that they express the same trait for which they judge someone else for. Every client I have worked with has experienced the same thing. In the first of the process questions, you will be asked to write down where you have expressed this trait. I guarantee that you have done so many times. You must be willing to look. The Ego wants to prove itself right and wants to avoid pain, so this can be challenging. Welcome to 'doing the work'.

What Is Trauma?

To summarise everything that has been said so far:

Trauma is a moment specific in time when something was too much or not enough. Trauma is broken down into specific words. Use one word to describe what happened, it will be a trait, action or inaction.

Examples:

Too much:

- Abuse

- Rejection
- Criticism
- Embarrassment
- Invalidation
- Aggression

Not enough:

- Love
- Safety
- Validation
- Presence
- Support
- Recognition
- Heard
- Seen

Balancing Perceptions Summary:

1. Every emotion you experience outside of love and gratitude is feedback of a lopsided perception.

2. Trauma is a moment in time when you created a lopsided perception, and the Balancing Process brings lopsided perceptions into balance.

3. Every single human being expresses all traits.

It's now time for you to prep for doing the Balancing Process. Let's do it.

Prep for the Process

Read through and understand the complete process. Reading all of the steps can seem like a lot, but using the Balancing Sheet from page 215 will make things so much easier. I'll also give you an example answer at the end of each question to help.

(The prep questions will be in *italics* and have a # in front of them in the table)

1. ***Decide on the person or event about whom/which you're going to do the process.***

Use these questions to help you:

- Who do I hold the most amount of judgement towards?

- Who has hurt me the most in life?

- Who would I not want to spend any time with?

- Who pushes my buttons the most?

- Who do I perceive as being in my way?

- Who is running my life or burdening me the most?

The higher the emotional charge, the greater the release/healing. To make things easier for doing the first process, I will guide you with who to choose, but remember you can do this process as many times as you like on anyone that you have emotional charge towards.

Example: *Father*

2. ***Find the specific trait, action or inaction (I will just say trait from now on to save repeating this each time) for which you judge this person. You must give only a one-word answer.***

When you judge someone, it's not EVERYTHING about them that you judge. It's a specific trait, action or inaction.

Also, a tip for doing this process without a facilitator/coach: I would avoid the 'Big T Traumas': rape, war, severe childhood abuse, witnessing death, etc, to start with. However, once you've done this process a couple of times and you feel confident, please do so.

Here is a list of common traits/actions/inactions that work well in doing this process:

- Lying
- Dismissive
- Stubborn
- Arrogance
- Selfish
- Jealous
- Insensitive
- Unreliable
- Entitled
- Condescending
- Greed
- Disrespect
- Weak
- Soft
- Violent
- Anger
- Gossip

- Careless

- Impatience

- Suppressing

- Invalidating

- Unsafe

- Lazy

- Perfectionist

- Needy

- Overbearing

- Resentment

- Disloyal

- Coward

- Manipulating

- Criticising

- Addictive

- Cruel

- Aggressive

- Belittling

Example: _Father, Aggressive._

3. Find a specific moment when you saw this person displaying this trait.

Make sure this is not based on what someone else has told you.

Make sure it's something you have seen and experienced through your own eyes.

Example: *My dad punched down the door to get to my brother and hurt him.*

4. Write down the opposite of this trait.

In that moment when they were doing the trait that you didn't want, what were you wanting from them?

Example: *Opposite of aggressive: Loving.*

5. Write down your top three Values.

Go back and review your top three Values before doing this process.

Example: *Coaching, learning, relationships.*

Steps for doing the process

1.

a. **Write down all the times in your life where you have expressed the same trait.** Look in the seven areas of life – spiritual, mental, vocational, financial, familial, social, physical. The trait will be in different forms – and look within your Values. Do not move on until you see and recognise that you express the same trait to the same degree that this other person does. Write down the person who saw you do it, a date and a location as a reference. You need at least 20 references. You can have the same person more than once.

Example of all the times I've displayed the trait of aggressive: *Brother – home 2015. Georgia – kitchen last week. Mr Thompson – classroom 2007. Sister – mum's house 2023. My ex-partner – her house 2017. Mum – home 2010. Jake – school 2012. Rory – playground 2017. Adam – school 2012. Georgia – couch last month. Dad – phone call last week. Brother – football game 2013. Georgia – pizza place 2022. Georgia – Christmas 2022. Scott – PLC*

Burleigh 2020. Jen – PLC Coomera 2019. Dad – football 2013. Georgia – table today. Ethan – school 2008. Dad – his house 2022.

b. **Can you recognise that you display this trait to the same degree as this person (probably in different forms)?** If the answer is no, go back and find more moments of you displaying this trait until the answer is yes. Once you can genuinely say yes, move on to the next question.

Example: *Yes*

2.

a. **Write down everything this person (the person on whom you're doing the process) has gone through for them to be displaying this trait.** Think of their childhood, their parents, their own traumas and conditioning.

Example: *My dad went through his own trauma in his upbringing, having his own father who didn't teach him how to regulate his emotions. He had never had the opportunity to do his healing work because he was never exposed to it. He had so many unhealed things that he carried around with him every day.*

b. **Can you understand why this person displayed this trait?** This doesn't mean that you agree with what they did, but you can understand why. To understand is to forgive. If you can't say yes, go back to the previous question and keep writing. Once you can genuinely say yes, move on to the next question.

Example: *Yes.*

3.

a. **What emotions did this person experience going through what they went through (what you just wrote down in the previous answer)?** Minimum of eight emotions.

Example: _Fear, anxiety, frustration, resentment, loneliness, anger, shame, guilt._

b. **Close your eyes and feel each of those emotions one by one.** Make the feeling a 10/10. The healing is in the feeling.

4.

a. **What are the benefits to you because of them displaying that trait to you?** This can be hard to answer if there is a lot of emotional charge towards this person and this trait. Keep going until you recognise that there are just as many benefits (+) as there are drawbacks (-) to this trait. Do at least 20 benefits.

(Hot tips: Look within your Values and the seven areas of life. Another way to ask the question: _What did I need to summon within myself to overcome them displaying this trait?_ Using one word answers helps.)

Example: _The benefits to me for my dad being aggressive: Helped me regulate my emotions. More empathy for my dad. Has made me a better father for the future. Has made me a better partner. I set firm boundaries. It's given me strength. Resilience. Courage. Helped me start my healing journey. It's made me a better coach for my clients. Compassion. Firmness. Forgiveness. Understanding. Loving. Resourcefulness. Connection. Leadership. Focus. Assertiveness._

b. **Would you give up these gifts?** If your answer is yes, go back and find more benefits to the previous question. Once you can genuinely say no, move on to the next question.

Example: _No._

5.

a. **If someone were to give you those gifts (from the previous question) what emotions would you feel?** Minimum five emotions.

Example: *Gratitude. Love. Joy. Thankfulness. Appreciation.*

b.   Recognising that this person (whom you're doing this process on) gifted you with all of these gifts. Close your eyes and feel those emotions one by one towards this person.

6.

Quickly read over all the gifts you received in question 4.

We get taught things in two ways – we get given what someone has, or we get given what they don't have.

You were given these gifts because this person (the person on whom you're doing this process) didn't have them to the level they wanted them. This person wanted them so badly, that's why they gifted them to you. You are the greatest gift.

See that and feel that now. Once you REALLY see and feel this, move on to the next question.

7.

a.   Where has this person displayed the opposite trait (#4 from the prep questions)? Write down the person who saw them do it, a date and a location as a reference. Keep going until you recognise that this person displays this trait just as much as the one you despised in them. Minimum 20 references.

Example: *Opposite trait; Loving. Where has my dad displayed loving? Me - football 2013. Me - my room 2010. Me - car my birthday. Sister - Christmas 2010. Brother - Christmas 2010. Sister - home 2008. Me - home 2007. Me - farm 2010. Georgia - wedding 2024. Me - kitchen 2023. Sister - graduation 2011. Me - bathroom 2024. Nan - nan's 2020. Me - kitchen 2020. Brother - school 2012. Brother - football 2011. Me - Brisbane 2012. Mum - home 2009. Sister - home 2008. Me - Tbar 2011.*

b. **Can you recognise that this person displays both of these traits to the same degree (probably in different forms)?** If your answer is no, go back and find more references of them displaying the opposite trait. Once you can genuinely say yes, move on to the next question.

Example: _Yes._

8.

a. **In that moment (#3 from the prep questions), if this person displayed the opposite trait (#4 of the prep questions), what would be the drawbacks to you?** Minimum 20.

(Hot tip: look within your Values.)

Example: _If my dad was loving in that moment instead of aggressive, what would the drawbacks be? Weaker. No boundaries. No grit. Less empathy. Less hunger. Less independence. Disconnection (from brother). Less intuition. Less passion. Not relatable. Needy. Less vulnerability. No growth. Less understanding (of dad). Unconfident. Less courage. Attached. Less healing. Less emotional intelligence. Less presence._

b. Can you recognise that both traits (#2 and #4 from the prep questions) have just as many drawbacks to them? If your answer is no, go back and add more drawbacks. Once you can genuinely say yes, move on to the next question.

Example: _Yes._

9.

a. **Look at all the gifts from question 4. Ultimately, who did this person help you become? Use an <u>adjective</u> and an <u>archetype</u>.**

(Examples: Integrated Father. Strong Mother. Brave Husband. Caring Woman. Loving Leader)

Example: *A balanced father.*

b. Can you see, feel and understand that this person played the role they were meant to play, to help you become who you were born to be? If your answer is no, go back and add to all of the questions. Once you can genuinely say yes, move on to the final question.

Example: *Yes.*

10. Write a letter of gratitude to this person.

Example: *Dear Dad,*

Thank you for doing the best with what you had. Thank you for gifting me with the strength, resilience, patience and emotional intelligence that I have. Thank you for helping me to start my healing journey, I wouldn't have done the work I've done on myself if it wasn't for you. Thank you for helping me become the father that I want to become. I wouldn't be the man, the coach, the father and the partner I am today if it wasn't for everything you did for me. Thank you.

That's the process! I'd recommend reading through the process more than once to get your head around it. Also, see on the next page what a completed table from doing the process looks like. I have filled the table with the examples I gave in the previous questions.

(Note: Because of the depth that this process goes into, about 40% of it has been left out, because it would become too difficult to communicate and facilitate the entire process in a book. The full process is available in my other services.)

My Process Example

#1. Name of person I'm balancing:	#2. What's the trait I judge the most in this person?	#3. What is a specific moment of this person displaying this trait?	#4. What is the opposite of this trait?	#5. My top three Values:
Dad	Aggressive	My dad punched down the door to get to my brother and hurt him.	Loving	1. Coaching. 2. Learning 3. Relationships
1. a) Where have I expressed this trait in my life? Minimum of 20.	2. a) What did this person go through for them to display this trait?	3. a) What emotions did this person experience going through what they went through? Minimum of 8.	4. a) What are the benefits to you because of them displaying that trait to you? Minimum of 20.	5. a) What emotions would I feel if someone gifted you with these gifts? Minimum of five.
1. Brother – home – 2015 2. Georgia – kitchen – last week 3. Mr Thompson – classroom – 2007 4. Sister – Mum's house – 2023 5. Ex-partner – her house – 2017 6. Mum- home – 2010 7. Jake – school – 2012 8. Rory – playground – 2017 9. Adam – school – 2012 10. Georgia – couch – last month 11. Dad – phone call – last week 12. Brother – football game – 2013 13. Georgia – pizza place – 2022 14. Georgia – Christmas – 2022 15. Scott – PLC Burleigh – 2020 16. Jen – PLC Coomera – 2019 17. Dad – football – 2023 18. Georgia – table – today 18. Ethan – school – 2008 19. Dad – home – 2022 20. Georgia – kitchen – last week	My dad went through his own trauma in his upbringing. Having a father who didn't teach him how to regulate his emotions. He never had the opportunity to do his healing work because he was never exposed to it. He had so many unhealed things that he carried around with him every single day.	1. Fear 2. Anxiety 3. Frustration 4. Resentment 5. Loneliness 6. Anger 7. Shame 8. Guilt	1. Regulate my emotions 2. Empathy 3. Better father in the future 4. Better partner 5. Firm boundaries 6. Strength 7. Resilience 8. Courage 9. Healing journey 10. Better coach 11. Compassion 12. Firmness 13. Forgiveness 14. Understanding 15. Loving 16. Resourcefulness 17. Connection 18. Leadership 19. Focus 20. Assertiveness	1. Gratitude 2. Love 3. Joy 4. Thankfulness 5. Appreciation
	b) Can you understand why they displayed this trait? Yes	b) Feel those emotions one by one.		
b) Can you recognise that you display this trait to the same degree as this person? Yes			b) Would you give up these gifts? No	b) Feel those emotions one by one towards this person.

214

6.	7.	8.	9.
Quickly read over the gifts you received in question 4.	(a) Where has this person displayed the opposite trait (#4 from the prep questions)? Minimum of 20.	(a) In that moment (#3 from the prep questions), if this person displayed the opposite trait (#4 of the prep questions), what would the drawbacks be to you? Minimum of 20.	(a) Look at all the gifts from question 4. Ultimately, who did this person help you to become? An adjective and an archetype.
We get taught things in two ways – we get given what someone has, or we get given what they don't.	1. Me – football – 2013 2. Me – my room – 2010 3. Me – my car – on birthday 4. Sister – Christmas – 2010 5. Brother – Christmas – 2010 6. Sister – home – 2008 7. Me – home – 2007 8. Me – farm – 2010 9. Georgia – wedding – 2024 10. Me – kitchen – 2023 11. Sister – graduation – 2011 12. Me – bathroom – 2024 13. Nan – her house – 2020 14. Me – kitchen – 2020 15. Brother – school – 2012 16. Brother – football – 2011 17. Me – Brisbane – 2012 18. Mum – home – 2009 19. Sister – home – 2008 20. Me – Tbar - 2011	1. Weaker 2. No boundaries 3. No grit 4. Less empathy 5. Less hunger 6. Less independence 7. Disconnection 8. Less intuition 9. Less passion 10. Less relatable 11. Needy 12. Less vulnerability 13. No growth 14. Less understanding 15. Unconfident 16. Less courage 17. Attached 18. Less healing 19. Less emotional intelligence 20. Less presence	A balanced father
You were given these gifts because this person didn't have them to the level they wanted them. They wanted them so badly. That's why they gifted them to you. YOU ARE THE GREATEST GIFT.	b) Can you recognise that this person displays both traits to the same degree?	b) Can you recognise that both traits have just as many drawbacks to them?	b) Can you see, feel and understand this person played the role they were meant to play, to help you become who you were born to be?
See that and feel that now.	Yes	Yes	Yes

10. *Letter of gratitude:*

> Dear Dad,
>
> Thank you for doing the best with what you had. Thank you for gifting me with the strength, resilience, patience and emotional intelligence that I have. Thank you for helping me to start my healing journey, I wouldn't have done the work I've done on myself if it wasn't for you. Thank you for helping me become the father that I want to become. I wouldn't be the man, the coach, the father and the partner I am today if it wasn't for everything you did for me. Thank you.

The time has finally come for you to do the process. Take time to read and see how to answer the questions from the example that I've provided.

Before you start, here are my top tips:

Tips for this process:

1. Make sure you have scheduled enough time to do the complete process – at least two or even three hours. If possible, don't have anything else planned for the rest of the day from when you start.

2. You will hit 'the wall' many times through this process. Remove all distractions. Your Ego wants to avoid pain and wants to prove itself right, so it will try to distract you from doing this healing process. Some questions will be very hard to answer, but you always can if you push through the resistance (the wall). Put the phone away. Tell everyone to leave you alone. Focus.

3. Make sure you're regulating your emotions throughout the process. However, when you're told to 'feel those emotions one by one' do that at the highest level you can. Get to a 10/10 level.

4. Do not move on until you have done the minimum number of answers or have answered the 'correct' yes/no questions.

5. Do not just 'tick the box', do this process to the best of your ability. It will change your life.

6. If it gets too much for you during the process, stop and revisit it when you're ready.

7. I have made a video and an online version of the Balancing Sheet which can make this process easier for you. Go to www.lewishuckstep.com/book or scan this

Let's begin.

The Balancing Process

Prep Questions:

1. Take a deep breath in. Calm your mind as much as you can. Answer this question as honestly and authentically as you can: *Which parent do you dislike or despise the most?*

   *This is the person on whom you are going to do the process. This doesn't mean that you don't love this person, you might have a great relationship with this parent. But answer that question honestly. If you didn't have parents growing up, use whoever played the carer role for you or who comes to mind when you read that question. If you struggle to answer the question, reword the question to "Which parent do I like the least?" Add this person's name into #1 of the prep questions on the Balancing Sheet on TABLE 6.

2. You can only use a one-word answer: *What trait/action/ inaction do you dislike or despise the most about them?*

Go back to page 215 for a list of traits if you're struggling to get it into one word. Once you have your word, add this into #2 of the prep questions on the Balancing Sheet.

3. *What is a specific moment of this person displaying this trait?*

Add this answer into #3 of the prep questions on the Balancing Sheet. Make sure that this is a specific moment that you experienced/witnessed it happening yourself, not what someone else has told you.

4. *What is the opposite of this trait?*

One-word answer. Add this answer into #4 of the prep questions on the Balancing Sheet.

5. *What are your top three Values?*

Add these answers into #5 of the prep questions on the Balancing Sheet.

The Process questions: (Read these questions out loud to yourself.)

1.

    a. **Write down all the times in your life where you have expressed the same trait.** Look in all seven areas of life areas of life – spiritual, mental, vocational, financial, familial, social, physical – and look within your Values. Do not move on until you see and recognise that you express the same trait to the same degree that this other person does. Write down the person who saw you do it, a date and a location as a reference. You need at least 20 references. You can have the same person more than once.

    b. Can you recognise that you display this trait to the same degree as this person? Probably in different forms. If the answer is no, go back & find more moments of you displaying this trait until the answer is yes. Once you can genuinely say yes, move on to the next question.

2.

    a. Write down everything this person (the person on whom you're doing the process) has gone through for them to be displaying this trait. Think of their childhood, their parents, their own traumas & conditioning.

    b. Can you understand why they displayed this trait? This doesn't mean that you agree with what they did, but you can understand why. To understand is to forgive. If you can't say yes, go back to the previous question and keep writing. Once you can genuinely say yes, move on to the next question.

3.

    a. What emotions did this person experience going through what they went through (what you just wrote down in the previous answer)? Minimum of eight emotions.

    b. Close your eyes and feel each of those emotions one by one. Make the feeling a 10/10. The healing is in the feeling.

4.

    a. What are the benefits to you because of them displaying that trait to you? This can be hard to answer if there is a lot of emotional charge towards this person and this trait. Keep going until you recognise that there are just as many benefits (+) as there are drawbacks (-) to this trait. Do at least 20 benefits.

    (Hot tips: Look within your Values and the 7 areas of life. Another way to ask the question: <u>What did I need to</u>

summon within myself to overcome them displaying this trait? Using one-word answers helps.)

b. **Would you give up these gifts (benefits)?** If you say yes, go back and add more benefits to the previous question. Once you can genuinely say no, move on to the next question.

5.

a. **If someone were to give you those gifts, what emotions would you feel?** Minimum 5 emotions.

b. **Recognise that this person (whom you're doing this process on) gifted you with all of these gifts.** Close your eyes and feel those emotions one by one towards this person.

6. **Quickly read over all the gifts you received in question 4.**

We get taught things in two ways – we get given what someone has, or we get given what they don't have.

You were given these gifts because this person (the person on whom you're doing this process) didn't have them to the level they wanted them. This person wanted them so badly, that's why they gifted them to you. You are the greatest gift.

See that and feel that now. Once you REALLY see and feel this, move on to the next question.

7.

a. **Where has this person displayed the opposite trait (#4 from the prep questions)?** Write down the person who saw them do it, a date and a location as a reference. Keep going until you recognise that this person displays this trait just as much as the one you despised in them. Minimum 20 references.

b. **Can you recognise that this person displays both of these traits to the same degree? In different forms.** If your answer is no, go back & find more references of them displaying the opposite trait. Once you can genuinely say yes, move on to the next question.

8.

a. **In that moment (#3 from the prep questions), if this person displayed the opposite trait (#4 of the prep questions), what would be the drawbacks to you?** Minimum 20.

Hot tip: Look within your Values and the 7 areas of life.

b. **Can you recognise that both traits (#2 & #4 from the prep questions) have just as many drawbacks to them?** If your answer is no, go back & add more drawbacks. Once you can genuinely say yes, move on to the next question.

9.

a. **Look at all the gifts from question 4. Ultimately, who did this person help you become?** An <u>adjective</u> and an <u>archetype</u>. Example: Integrated Father. Strong Mother. Brave Husband. Caring Woman. Loving Leader

b. **Can you see, feel and understand that this person played the role they were meant to play, to help you become who you were born to be?** If your answer is no, go back and add to all of the questions. Once you can genuinely say yes, move on to the final question.

10. **Once you have completed the process, write a letter of gratitude to this person. (You will find a space to do this after TABLE 6)**

TABLE 6 – Balancing Sheet

#1. Name of person I'm balancing:	#2. What's the trait I judge the most in this person?	#3. What is a specific moment of this person displaying this trait?	#4. What is the opposite of this trait?	#5. My top three Values:
1. a) Where have I expressed this trait in my life? Minimum of 20.	2. a) What did this person go through for them to display this trait?	3. a) What emotions did this person experience going through what they went through? Minimum of 8.	4. a) What are the benefits to <u>you</u> because of them displaying that trait to you? Minimum of 20.	5. a) What emotions would I feel if someone gifted you with these gifts? Minimum of five.
b) Can you recognise that you display this trait to the same degree as this person?	b) Can you understand why they displayed this trait?	b) Feel those emotions one by one.	b) Would you give up these gifts?	b) Feel those emotions one by one towards this person.

6.	7.	8.	9.
Quickly read over the gifts you received in question 4.	(a) Where has this person displayed the opposite trait (#4 from the prep questions)? Minimum of 20.	(a) In that moment (#3 from the prep questions), if this person displayed the opposite trait (#4 of the prep questions), what would the drawbacks be to you? Minimum of 20.	(a) Look at all the gifts from question 4. Ultimately, who did this person help you to become? An adjective and an archetype.
You were given these gifts because this person didn't have them to the level they wanted them. They wanted them so badly. That's why they gifted them to you. YOU ARE THE GREATEST GIFT.	b) Can you recognise that this person displays both traits to the same degree?	b) Can you recognise that both traits have just as many drawbacks to them?	b) Can you see, feel and understand this person played the role they were meant to play, to help you become who you were born to be?
See that and feel that now.			

Letter of gratitude:

_____

_____

_____

_____

_____

_____

_____

_____

_____

_____

_____

_____

_____

_____

_____

WELL DONE!!!

What a process. Congratulations for doing the work and following through with this. If you did this process correctly, you will have had a lot of emotional releases and rebalancing of your perceptions, and experienced a lot more love and gratitude for the person on whom you did this process.

If you've ever heard the quote 'Life is happening FOR you not TO you', what you just went through was how you can truly see and feel that.

If you haven't already, once you finish going through a process like this, take time to recharge and integrate yourself. You've literally shifted a perception of someone about whom you've had a high emotional charge for years, if not decades.

If you struggled with the process and didn't have the shifts you were wanting, that's okay. You always receive what you're ready to receive. I'd recommend doing the process again when you're ready to. Keep in mind about 40% of this process has been left out because of the limitations of teaching it in a book. Maybe you're needing the full experience. You'll learn how you can get that at the end of the book.

This is the result after completing this process on my dad with the example I shared with you :

After completing this process on my dad, I felt really light, I felt love and I had so much gratitude for him. Two days later, I happened to be driving him to the airport. My entire life to that point, whenever I was with my dad, I had felt anxious around him (traumatic reaction). That day I drove him to the airport was the first time in my entire life that I felt safe around him. Why? Not because he acted any differently to the way he normally does, but because I had healed the wound within myself that was there from him. Our relationship continues to get better and better, the more healing I do.

Extra tips for the Balancing Process:

- You will have many different wounds with the same person.
- Schedule time into your calendar to do a process regularly. No more than one per week is a recommendation.

- Use The Trigger Hit List to help you find what wounds to do a process on.

Motivation to Continue Your Inner Work

If you ever needed motivation to do your own Inner Work, this is it.

Whatever you judge (have a lopsided perception about) you will attract. You will be triggered by it and you continue to do this until you heal (balance) it.

Your mind has something called the Reticular Activating System (RAS), which basically finds things that you deem as important. Think about when you wanted or purchased a new car, you saw that car everywhere. When you wanted or got a new piece of clothing, you saw that clothing everywhere.

However, it also works in reverse.

If I tell you to not look for a yellow bus, what are you thinking of? A yellow bus.

So if you have an unhealed trauma (lopsided perception), you're going to be unconsciously (or consciously) trying to avoid it. But you end up attracting it and being triggered by it.

What you run away from, you run into.

This will happen a lot inside of intimate relationships. Do you know of anyone who attracted a partner who reflected their unhealed wounds? The person who didn't want to date a narcissist because they have been hurt from a narcissist before, yet they attract another one? Something to think about...

So, whoever or whatever you have judgement towards, do the Balancing Process on that person and trait so you stop attracting it and being triggered by it.

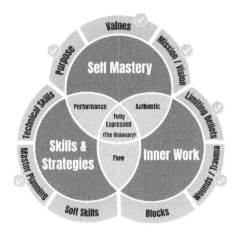

Figure 44

So close to the finish line!!!

We're almost finished working through all the pieces of *The Inspired Life Method* that I wanted to share in this book. There is one more piece to go, but before we get into it, I want to show you something that you can use both the Ego Dissolving Process and the Balancing Process in the best way possible moving forwards.

How to use this:

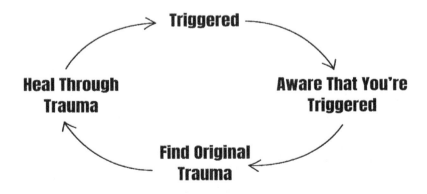

Figure 45

The aim of the game is to bring awareness of your own triggers, find the wound (trauma or lopsided perception), then heal through it.

The Trigger Hit List

1. Become aware that you're triggered or that you're judging something within someone (you don't like someone for some reason).

2. Determine if it is a limiting belief or trauma being revealed. Then ask yourself:

   a. What is the specific trait that triggered me, or that I'm judging this person for? It must be a one-word answer.

   b. What limiting belief is being triggered?

3. Write the person's name or the event, the date and the trait or the limiting belief into the table.

4. Write down which process you will use:

   a. If it is a trait, do the Balancing Process

   b. If it is a limiting belief, do the Ego Dissolving Process

5. Set aside time to do your own healing work.

Here is a simple table for you to fill in:

Name of Person or Event:	Specific Trait or Limiting Belief:	Date:	Ego Dissolving or Balancing Process
Dad	Criticising	05/10/2024	Balancing Process
Work Meeting	I'm stupid	07/10/2024	Ego Dissolving

You now have real ways of doing your own healing work. Pretty cool, right? Again, I recommend that you don't do a process more than once per week. Giving yourself time and space to integrate the work is very important.

Now I want to gift you with one more tool for you to:

1. Become the person worthy of your Vision and to manifest it.

2. Continue to do your Inner Work to help you heal and process mental/emotional blocks.

This tool is responsible for creating (manifesting) dream jobs/business opportunities. Attracting dream partners into people's lives. Healing through life-threatening 'incurable' conditions, such as cancer, autoimmune disease, PTSD, spinal cord injuries + MUCH more. I have been using this particular tool for the past seven years and it's completely changed my life. Let's get into it...

CHAPTER 12

Meditation - Remove Blocks

Change Your Personality and You'll Change Your Personal Reality

*"Thoughts are the language of the mind;
emotions are the language of the body."*
- Dr Joe Dispenza

Anna felt as though the gates of hell had closed on her. Western medicine had not only failed her but had also made the problems worse. Nine years before, she had been diagnosed with bipolar disorder, anxiety, depression and PTSD. Over the years, she had been treated by multiple psychiatrists and prescribed numerous psychiatric medications. Last year, the side effects of these medications began to outweigh their benefits, leading her to a critical decision: she would come off the psychiatric medications.

With the guidance of her doctor, Anna carefully and slowly came off the medications; however, within weeks she experienced a severe reaction. Her nervous system went into shock and became completely dysregulated, leaving her unable to sleep and in a constant state of panic for three long months.

Experts informed Anna that her condition couldn't be fixed or undone with any pharmaceutical medicine. It would take an unknown amount of time for her body to heal but they could make no promises.

Any attempt to help with medications would likely worsen her condition.

In her desperation, Anna stumbled upon the book "*Becoming Supernatural.*" She read it in two days and began practicing the meditations three times a day, every day. She focused solely on healing, on changing her emotional state by feeling empowering emotions. She visualized herself getting through this challenge and emerging on the other side.

Despite the daunting conditions — experts told her recovery could take six to 18 months — Anna's dedication to her meditation practice worked. In just twelve weeks, she experienced a profound shift. The panic left her, and she was able to sleep again. Her nervous system came back to normal, and she no longer suffered from any symptoms.

Nine months later, Anna remained free from any symptoms of bipolar disorder, anxiety, depression, PTSD or any other mental health issues. She was completely healed. Showing that when you change your emotions (remove emotional blocks), you heal.

How to Use Meditation to Heal and Create

Dr Joe Dispenza is one of the leading minds in the world and in history when it comes to human transformation. It is hard to believe some of the transformations that he has facilitated for his clients, but they're happening every single day.

Here are just some of the types of transformation he's achieving with his clients:

- Healing cancer

- Healing autoimmune disease

- Healing infertility

- Healing IBS

- Overcoming chronic fatigue

- Healing spinal cord injuries

- Curing Crohn's disease

- Healing trauma - PTSD

- Healing Hashimoto's disease

- Overcoming anorexia

- Healing erectile dysfunction

- Overcoming stuttering

- Curing blindness

- Curing deafness

- Healing OCD

- Healing depression

- Healing anxiety

- Healing chronic pains

- And so much more...

Dr Joe's work is incredibly deep, and he has all the research and data from: multiple bestselling books, many research papers, tens of thousands of brain scans and much more. I won't do Dr Joe's work any justice trying to explain the depth of what he does for people, but I will touch on a couple of key points that we can use to help with our healing and growth journey together. Please do yourself a favour: read his books and dive into his world of wisdom and transformation.

One part of Dr Joe's work that I'd like to pass onto you, and that ties into *The Inspired Life Method*, is the teaching that comes from the quote at the start of this chapter.

"Thoughts are the language of the mind; emotions are the language of the body."

Let's break that down a little bit more. There's something called the Thinking Feeling Loop, which simply explains the relationship between thoughts and feelings, as well as the reinforcing relationship they have with each other.

Negative thinking feeling loop:

- You think a negative thought.

- That triggers a negative feeling.

- That negative feeling brings on more negative thoughts.

- Those additional negative thoughts trigger more negative feelings.

We've all experienced this before, and it sucks.

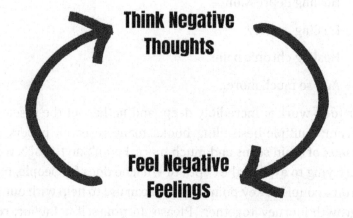

Figure 46

However, it works in the positive direction as well.

- You think a positive thought.
- That triggers a positive feeling.
- That positive feeling brings on more positive thoughts.

- Those additional positive thoughts trigger more positive feelings.

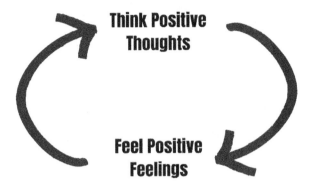

Figure 47

Pretty straight forward right? So just think positive thoughts and you'll feel positive? Not so simple. Understand this:

An emotion is the end product of an experience – If you experience something bad, you feel bad.

Your mind doesn't know the difference between an experience it's having in real life and thinking about the memory of an experience. You think about something bad, you feel bad.

Every single thought and experience is linked to an emotion.

You think between 60,000 to 70,000 thoughts every single day and 90% of those thoughts are the same thoughts from the previous day. You think the same thoughts, you feel the same emotions. You keep copying and pasting your days over and over again.

In fact, by the age of 35, 95% of what you do every single day is subconscious – you're on autopilot. Only 5% of what you do each day are conscious decisions.

Additionally, your body over time becomes addicted to the emotions that it's used to feeling every single day: the stress, the dopamine, the worry, the anxiety. Your body literally is conditioned and is addicted to feeling those emotions.

If every single day you're thinking the same negative thoughts and you're feeling the same negative emotions, this leads to the same decisions and actions. You're literally trapped in your own program of familiar thoughts and feelings.

So, you can say with your 5% conscious mind - I want to be healthy, I want to be wealthy, I want to be happy, as much as you want, but you're fighting a losing battle against the 95% unconscious mind and the body which is addicted to those familiar emotions.

So how do you solve this? Great question. There's many tools to do so, and this book has given you some of them; however, the one Dr Joe mainly uses is meditation.

Now, as soon as I first heard the word meditation, I instantly rejected it. The thought of sitting down and trying to think about nothing didn't exactly sound like fun to me; however, once I understood the power of meditation and I experienced how much it can help to heal and transform, I was hooked.

Another massive shift that I got from Dr Joe's work was his teachings on how to achieve goals/manifestation.

Here's how most people think: *Once I achieve a certain goal - a house, a number in my bank account, a level of success in my business or career, a follower amount, a loving relationship, etc., then I'll feel a certain emotion - happiness, love, gratitude, joy, etc.*

That's an outdated & incorrect way of thinking. Here's Dr Joe's view on this:

Get so clear on what it is that you want to achieve - a house, a number in your bank account, a level of success in your business or career, a follower amount, a loving relationship, etc, and then get clear on what emotion you will feel once you've achieved that goal - happiness, love, gratitude, joy etc. But feel those emotions NOW and you will attract those goals into your life.

Don't wait to achieve your goals to feel positive emotions. Instead, feel the positive emotions now and then you'll attract/achieve your goals a lot easier.

"To change your personal reality,
you need to change your personality."
- Dr Joe Dispenza.

If you want to change your personal reality, you're going to have to change your personality. In other words, change those subconscious beliefs (95% of your beliefs, remember) and condition your body to a new emotional home to stop you going into a negative thinking, feeling loop anymore. This is another way of saying - you have to remove the mental and emotional blocks that are stopping you from creating the life you deserve. This is why Blocks are a part of *The Inspired Life Method*.

Meditation is so powerful because:

1. You can rewrite those deep unconscious beliefs.

2. You can recondition your body to a new emotional home by consciously practicing the feeling of positive emotions.

3. It allows you to process your thoughts. Remember trauma is unprocessed memories (unprocessed experiences).

(Side note - there are so many other benefits of meditation, we're just focusing on these for now.)

The two types of meditation that I want to introduce to you are:

1. Creation and change: get very clear on what you want – your vision/intention, and then practice feeling the positive

emotions linked to that vision/intention, to condition your body to that positive emotion.

2. Processing and healing: giving yourself the space to process any thoughts that want to be processed. Also go through the Ego Dissolving Process or the Balancing Process in your own time and at your own pace (once you've done those two processes enough times, you'll know them well enough to ask yourself the questions).

I have created these two meditations for free that you can access from my website: www.lewishuckstep.com/book. If you don't have access to that, that's okay. I've included the meditations for you, so you can read through it and practice them at your own pace.

(Hot tip - If you can play some healing frequencies as you read these, it will enhance the experience. (You'll find plenty on YouTube or Spotify).

Instructions for completing the book version of the Creation and Changing Meditation:

1. Read over your Vision to refresh yourself.

2. Do some slow relaxing breathwork before starting - 5, 5, 5 breathing is perfect.

3. Read one line, then close your eyes and allow your mind to answer or sit with what you read. When it feels right, open your eyes and move onto the next line.

4. Repeat until finished.

Creation and Changing Meditation:

Take a deep breath in.

Bring your awareness to your heart.

Breathe into your heart.

Feel the strength of your heart.

Now, see and feel a light around your heart. Start to grow stronger with every breath.

Breathe deep into your heart.

Now, see that light start to travel down the centre of your body, all the way to the bottom of your spine.

Now, see and feel strong roots start to grow from beneath you. Feel them grow through the floor, into the crust of the earth and all the way into the core of the earth.

With this connection to the earth below you, breathe in strength, power, groundedness and stability.

Now, as you continue your breath, I want you to see and feel a portal just above your head start to open.

Now, a white light from the centre of the universe shoots down: into that portal, into you and into your heart.

This light is intelligence. It is source. It is God, spirit or whatever word is right for you.

Feel this connection in your heart.

Now, what is your Vision for your future?

See that Vision now.

See it so clearly that it feels real.

Step into that Vision now.

Who is the version of yourself worthy of that Vision?

Be that person now.

What emotion does that version of you feel?

Feel that emotion now.

Double the intensity of that feeling.

Come on, open your heart and feel it.

Keep feeling it.

Stay present.

What thoughts does this version of you think?

Say them to yourself now.

What behaviours does this version of you do?

See yourself doing them now.

Bring your awareness back to your breath.

Take a moment to give yourself gratitude for being your beautiful self.

When you get up from this meditation, get up as the new version of you.

With the new feelings. The new thoughts. The new behaviours.

Step into your new life, as the new you.

Instructions for completing the book version of the Processing and Healing Meditation:

1. Think about a person or a situation that's been on your mind and you're wanting to process/heal.

2. Do some slow relaxing breathwork before starting - 5, 5, 5 breathing is perfect.

3. Read one line, then close your eyes and allow your mind to answer or sit with what you read. When it feels right, open your eyes and move onto the next line.

4. Repeat until finished.

Processing and Healing Meditation:

Take a deep breath in.

Bring your awareness to your heart.

Breathe into your heart.

Feel the strength of your heart.

Now, see and feel a light around your heart start to grow stronger with every breath.

Breathe deep into your heart.

Now, see that light start to travel down the centre of your body, all the way to the bottom of your spine.

Now, see and feel strong roots start to grow from beneath you. Feel them grow through the floor, into the crust of the earth and all the way into the core of the earth.

With this connection to the earth below you, breathe in strength, power, groundedness and stability.

Now as you continue your breath. I want you to see and feel a portal just above your head start to open.

Now, a white light from the centre of the universe shoots down: into that portal, into you and into your heart.

This light is intelligence. It is source. It is God, spirit or whatever word is right for you.

Feel this connection in your heart.

Now, what is that person or situation that's been on your mind?

Why is this showing up in your life for you?

What's the empowering lesson that it's there to teach you?

How will that lesson help you grow?

Why else is this showing up for you?

What else is this here to teach you?

What are the benefits of this happening for you?

What's another benefit?

Feel the gratitude and love of receiving those gifts.

Open your heart and feel it.

What would it feel like to be totally at peace with this?

Feel that now.

Take a deep breath in.

How would love respond to this?

See and feel that now.

Stay present.

Bring your awareness back to your breath.

Take a moment to give yourself gratitude for being your beautiful self.

When you get up from this meditation, get up as the new version of you.

With the new feelings. The new thoughts. The new behaviours.

Step into your new life, as the new you.

These meditations will change your life forever once you do them consistently. I'd recommend doing a minimum of four meditations per week, ideally one per day. This is how I decide which mediation to do:

1. If I feel like I'm not clear enough on where I'm going in life or I feel like I'm not being the best version of myself, I will do the Creation and Changing Meditation.

2. If I feel emotionally overwhelmed/drained or if I have a lot of thoughts going on in my head that I want to process/heal, I will do the Processing and Healing Meditation.

Meditation Summary:

1. Thoughts are the language of the mind; emotions are the language of the body.

2. To change your personal reality, you must change your personality, your thoughts and the emotional home of your body.

3. Meditation allows you to change your beliefs, change your body's emotional home and allows you to heal/process wounds.

Final status check:

Figure 48

Congratulations!!!

We have finished the final piece of *The Inspired Life Method* that we will be journeying together. The reason it's not fully complete is that the ways to teach the rest of the pillars, and the tools within the pillars, exceed what can be done within this book. It requires spreadsheets, videos and in-person experiences. Even some of the tools that we've gone through together in this book have been changed and shortened to work here. But don't worry, because in the coming pages I will be giving heaps of guidance on how you can complete the rest of the method and continue your growth journey.

Wrap It All Up/Summary

What a journey we've been on together. It's been a privilege to be a part of yours and hopefully I added some value to you along the way. I wanted to take the time to remind you of what we've journeyed through together with some quick notes for you to easily remember:

1. **Values**. These are the areas of your life that are intrinsically most important to you. If you're struggling with your self-worth, you're probably not prioritising your Values. Redo these every three months.

2. **Purpose**. This is your gift to give back to the world – an expression of your biggest core wound. Redo this every three months.

3. **Mission**. This is your BHAG (Big Hairy Audacious Goal). This is a big 5-10 goal that allows you to fulfil your Purpose. Redo this every three months.

4. **Vision**. This is what your life looks like once you've achieved your Mission. It's an expansion of your Values plus other areas that might not be in your Values right now. Redo and add to this every three months.

5. **Dream Life and income needed.** To live your Dream Life (your Vision) you now know what that life looks like and how much money you actually need to earn to live it.

6. **CashFlow Quadrant.** You now know the basic rules of money and the importance of using leverage to earn more money without using more time.

7. **Selecting the right vehicle.** Be aware of the pros and cons of each vehicle and make sure the vehicle you choose will allow you to earn the income you need for your Dream Life.

8. **Master Planning.** Breaking your Mission/Vision all the way down to daily action items. You now have clarity of how to

create your Vision. Redo this every three months and use the rhythms you were shown in this book.

9. **Unlimited Motivation.** This allows you to be motivated to do anything that needs to be done to fulfil your Vision. Just link benefits to your top three Values.

10. **Inner Healing.** Dissolving the wounds and blockages that are masking your true self. Inner Work never finishes. There is always more work to do. There are four bodies to heal through. They are Mental, Emotional, Physical and Spiritual (also Energetic plus other bodies, depending on who you talk to).

11. **Triggers, traumatic reactions, trauma.** Trauma is the event that happened or the time when your needs weren't met. A traumatic reaction is how you reacted to the trauma (coping mechanism). A trigger 'activates' the trauma and sets off the traumatic reaction. 'Nothing triggers you; it reveals what's inside of you.'

12. **Regulating Your Emotions.** You don't see things the way they are, you see things the way YOU are. Remember to be aware of when you're emotionally charged, then go straight into your 5, 5, 5 breathing to regulate yourself.

13. **Dissolving the Ego.** The Ego has two traits: 1. It will always prove itself right. 2. It will avoid pain. Your Authentic/True self is you without all the limitations that you've downloaded. The aim of the game is to find the limiting beliefs (Ego) and dissolve them, allowing your True Authentic Self to shine through.

14. **Balancing perceptions.** Everything we experience/see is a perception. When you experience a balanced perception (equal positives and negatives), you will feel gratitude and love. Anything that you can't say you're grateful and thankful for is due to a lopsided perception.

15. Meditation. Thoughts are the language of the mind. Emotions are the language of the body. To change your personal reality, you must change your personality. Use meditation to change your beliefs and your body's emotional home.

So now:

You know who you authentically are (Values and Purpose).

You know what you truly want (Mission and Vision).

You have clarity on what needs to get done for you to get there (Master Plan).

You also have tools in your toolbox to overcome the mental and emotional challenges that life is going to throw at you, as you pursue your Life's Vision.

You Are Ready

I want to thank you for going on this journey with me. This book is what I needed when I was just getting started, so I hope it has helped you to the level it would have helped me.

What's Next for You?

This is just one step along your path. There are many more steps to go. I encourage you to continue to invest in yourself to grow, to learn, to heal and to give back to others.

If you want to do further work with me, you can check out all my services at:

www.lewishuckstep.com

If you'd like to go deeper into the full version of *The Inspired Life Method*, which includes going into the specific skills and strategies needed to build a thriving business and relationship, as well as mastering your health, wealth and spirituality.

If you have received value from this book, it would mean the world to me if you could:

1. Leave a review. It will take less than two minutes.

2. Tell two friends about the book.

So, goodbye for now but not forever. Until we meet again.

Stay well. Follow what inspires you. Be aware of what triggers you. Do your inner work. Keep working on You.

With Love,

Lewis Huckstep.

Examples of My Values, Purpose, Mission, Vision:

Values:

1. *Coaching.*
2. *Relationships.*
3. *Learning.*
4. *Health.*
5. *Wealth.*
6. *Games.*
7. *Family.*

Purpose:

To Heal and Expand Consciousness.

Mission:

To coach 10 million people to live an Inspired Life.

Vision:

To keep things simple, I have just provided my Vision for my top three Values. Make sure you do all of yours plus the 'Other' areas of your Vision.

Value 1: *Coaching*

I am a highly desired, international keynote speaker. I work with inspiring high-quality clients who are prepared to invest in their own growth. I have global influence with my teaching. They create meaningful change. I have multiple programs that serve millions of people each year. I have written three bestselling books that have an impact on millions of people. I run in-person events with thousands of people attending each year. All my work creates real, life-changing results that have an impact on everyone with whom they come in contact. 'His work changed my life' is what people say about my coaching. I have contributed to raising this world's consciousness.

Value 2: _Relationships_

I have an incredibly intimate relationship with my partner. We support and challenge each other to grow into the people we want to become. We have absolute transparency with our communication which inspires other people to do the same. We both feel safe to be 100% vulnerable with each other and share any emotion that comes up. Our sex life is liberating and awakening; we explore all of our deepest desires together in a healthy way. We have beautiful, balanced children. We teach them life's lessons that allow them to create their Life's Vision. They understand open communication, how to be vulnerable, how to see both sides in anything and how to regulate their emotions. They inspire us both to be incredible role models.

Value 3: _Learning_

I have read more than 1000 books in the areas of human psychology, communication, leadership, consciousness, business and finances. I have attended any personal development program that inspires me to do so. I have learned from the world's greatest teachers. I have mastered my emotions and spirituality from the thousands of hours of self-work and meditation I've practised. I have documented my learnings to pass on to the world.

Master Plan:

Five-ten-year goal (Mission):

To coach 10 million people to live an inspired life.

Three-year goals:

1. _I am helping 5,000 people in my Conscious Community._

2. _I have one million people on my email list._

3. _I have written two bestselling books._

4. _I have run nationwide in-person tours a year._

5. _I have $5 million net worth._

Two-year goals:

1. *I am helping 2,000 people in my Conscious Community.*

2. *I have 100,000 people on my email list.*

3. *I have written and released one bestselling book.*

4. *I have run one nationwide in-person tour.*

5. *I have $2 million net worth.*

12-month goals:

1. *I am helping 500 in my Conscious Community.*

2. *I have 20,000 people on my email list.*

3. *I have published my first book.*

4. *I have run two in-person events.*

5. *I have $1 million net worth.*

Quarterly goals:

1. *I am helping 200 people in my Conscious Community.*

2. *I have 5,000 people on my email list.*

3. *I have finished writing and editing my first book (literally doing this right now).*

4. *I have finished all six chapters for my Conscious Community.*

5. *I have $350,000 net worth.*

Monthly goals:

1. *I am helping 120 people in my Conscious Community.*

2. *I have 4,000 people on my email list.*

3. *I have finished the first round of editing my book.*

4. *I have finished Chapter Two for my Conscious Community.*

5. *I have $250,000 net worth.*

Weekly goals:

1. *I am helping 100 people in my Conscious Community.*
2. *I have 3,800 people on my email list.*
3. *I have finished 80% of the first round of editing my book.*
4. *I have finished 80% of Chapter Two for my Conscious Community.*
5. *I have $240,000 net worth.*

Daily Huddle:

Step 1: What are you excited for today?

I'm excited about training, about writing my book and about my Masterclass tonight.

*Step 2: What were your outcomes for last week and were they done or not done? Why or why not? (This step is done only once per week; on a Monday morning or whatever day you start your week).

1. *I am helping 90 people in my Conscious Community – Done.* ✓
2. *I have 3,800 people on my email list – Not done.* ✗ *I didn't follow my normal posting schedule.*
3. *I have finished 80% of the first round of editing my book. – Done.* ✓
4. *I have finished 80% of Chapter Two for my Conscious Community. – Not done.* ✗ *I wasn't good enough with my focus levels.*
5. *I have $240,000 net worth. – Done.* ✓

Step 3: What were your outcomes for yesterday and were they done or not done? Why or why not?

1. *I have edited 5,000 words of my book – Done.* ✓
2. *I have had a full practice run over my Masterclass: The Purpose Process. – Done.* ✓

3. I have finished one module for Chapter Two of my Conscious Community. – Not done. ✗ I wasn't productive enough with my time.
4. I have completed Francine's and Sarah's coaching calls – Done. ✓
5. I have had one discovery call and made 1 sale. – Not done. ✗ I had the sales call, but I didn't close the sale.

Step 4: What are your outcomes to be completed today?

1. I have edited 5,000 words of my book.
2. I have run my Masterclass: The Purpose Process, with 100 people attending.
3. I have finished one module for Chapter Two of my Conscious Community.
4. I have sent out my weekly email blast to my email community.
5. I have booked in three discovery calls.

Step 5: Do you require support from anyone to complete these outcomes today?

No support needed.

Step 6: What are you grateful for today?

I'm grateful for my partner, my health and my clients.

Now it's your turn!

Values, Purpose, Mission, Vision

Values:

1. _____
2. _____
3. _____
4. _____
5. _____
6. _____
7. _____
8. _____

Purpose:

_____
_____
_____

Mission:

_____
_____
_____
_____

Vision:

Value 1:

_____

_____

_____

_____

_____

Value 2:

_____

_____

_____

_____

_____

Value 3:

_____

_____

_____

_____

Value 4:

_____

_____

_____

_____

_____

Value 5:

_____

_____

_____

_____

Value 6:

_____

_____

_____

_____

Value 7:

_____

_____

_____

_____

Other:

_____

_____

_____

_____

Your Master Plan: Five-ten-year goal (Mission):

_____

_____

_____

_____

Three-year goals:

1. _____
2. _____
3. _____
4. _____
5. _____

Two-year goals:

1. _____
2. _____
3. _____
4. _____
5. _____

12-month goals:

1. _____
2. _____
3. _____
4. _____
5. _____

Quarterly goals:

1. _____

2. _____

3. _____

4. _____

5. _____

Monthly goals:

1. _____

2. _____

3. _____

4. _____

5. _____

Weekly goals:

1. _____

2. _____

3. _____

4. _____

5. _____

Daily Huddle:

Step 1: What are you excited for today?

_____

_____

_____

_____

*Step 2: What were your outcomes for last week and were they done or not done? Why or why not? (This step is done only once a week ; on a Monday morning or whatever day you start your week).

1. _____

2. _____

3. _____

4. _____

5. _____

Step 3: What were your outcomes for yesterday and were they done or not done? Why or why not?

1. _____

2. _____

3. _____

4. _____

5. _____

Step 4: What are your outcomes to be completed today?

1. _____

2. _____

3. _____

4. _____

5. _____

Step 5: Do you require support from anyone to complete these outcomes today?

_____

_____

_____

_____

_____

Step 6: What are you grateful for today?

_____

_____

_____

_____

_____

ACKNOWLEDGEMENTS

This book would not be here today if it weren't for the countless number of people who played their role in my journey. I already made a list of mentors who have impacted my life in a meaningful way, so I won't be repeating their names. The mentions are the people who I know deeply on an intimate level.

Unfortunately, I can't name them all, but I want to thank a few special people.

Firstly, my wife, Georgia. Thank you for helping me grow into the man I am today and helping me heal through my wounds with love and strength. To show me what true unconditional love feels and looks like.

To both my parents, who gifted me with the perfect amount of challenge and support that I needed to become who I'm proud to be today.

My business and life coach Cody McAuliffe, without you I probably would have procrastinated writing this book for another three years. Thank you for initiating me into this journey and for all the impact you've made on my life.

My book coach, Tarryn Reeves, you helped me bring this gift to the world. I can't thank you enough for guiding me and helping me put this project together.

Of course, my beautiful clients, every single person who has ever trusted me as their coach, and whoever does so in the future. You allow me to live out my Purpose and give you my gift. Thank you.

Finally, I want to thank you for reading this book. I put over 1200 hours of my own time into writing and editing. I hope you received a great return on your investment of time and energy from this book. I hope you really use the tools provided in this book to become who you are destined to become. Be weird, be authentic, be you. Thank you.

About the Author

Lewis Huckstep is a dedicated fulfilment and performance coach specialising in helping leaders overcome self-sabotaging patterns. With a mission to heal through limitations, he enables clients to achieve greater external success and internal fulfilment, transforming achievers into visionaries.

Living by example, Lewis has built multiple successful businesses, both offline and online. Having coached over 3,500 people, reached millions through his social channels and is dedicated to his ongoing self-development and healing, Lewis understands how to develop and maintain a life of purpose, vision, and fulfilment.

Diagnosed with Asperger's, autism, and ADHD, Lewis's purpose is to heal and expand consciousness. His life's mission is to impact 10 million people, helping them live lives that inspire them. This book is one of the many ways he plans to achieve this goal. Lewis hopes this guide impacts you as profoundly as it has impacted him and his clients.

www.lewishuckstep.com

Made in the USA
Las Vegas, NV
29 October 2024

10642825R00154